Haunted

Tyler

And Beyond...

George Jones
Mitchel Whitington

ISBN
978-1-9393060-5-0

Library of Congress Control Number: 2014938116

First Edition

Printed in the United States of America
Published by 23 House Publishing
SAN 299-8084
www.23house.com

The paper used in this book meets the minimum requirements of the
American National Standard for Permanence of Paper for Printed Library
Materials, ANSI/NISO Z39.48-1992.
Binding materials have been chosen for durability.

This book is dedicated to our mothers,
Floye Nell Jones (12/3/1931 – 8/22/2009) and
Betty Jo Whitington (12/3/1928 - 6/27/2011)

Table of Contents

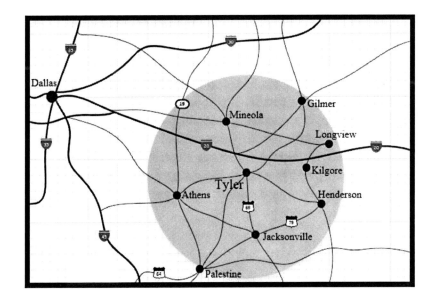

Welcome to Ghostly Tyler & Vicinity

Tyler is known as the "Rose Capital of the World" – it's a place of beauty and history, but the city and surrounding area are also a place of mystery, intrigue, and… ghosts!

Come along with your guides to discover the world of the supernatural. George Jones is a paranormal investigator, author, and owner of Jericho Tours which offers excursions around Tyler including several historic tours, a shopping tour, a ghost tour, and even active, overnight ghost hunts. He also presents Tyler's annual paranormal conference. Mitchel Whitington is a paranormal investigator as well, and an author who has visited, investigated, and written about some of the country's most notoriously haunted locations. Mitchel and his wife own The Grove, one of the most supernaturally active locations in the Lone Star State.

These two paranormal enthusiasts combine their talents to present the ultimate guide to the supernatural side of the Tyler area, writing in a singular voice to take you on a journey that you won't soon forget.

You'll find not only many haunted tales from the city itself, but others that are within a short drive if you care to visit them for yourself... that is, if you dare!

These aren't campfire ghost stories or local legends, but instead are locations with documented activity. You'll hear from some of the people who have experienced the spirits first-hand, including in some cases the authors themselves.

Sit back, dim the lights, and prepare for a ghostly experience!

Historic Tyler, Texas

The story of Tyler, the Rose Capital of the World, began back in the days when Texas was still a Republic and much of it was wild, untamed land. Independence from Mexico had been won in 1836, but there was soon a growing movement for Texas to join the United States of America – although there was controversy on both sides.

An overture to that effect was initially made in August of 1837, when Memucan Hunt, Jr., the Texas Minister to the United States proposed such an annexation to President Martin Van Buren. Unfortunately, the general feeling in the administration was that with any such plan, the U.S. would inherit Texas' hostilities with Mexico, which in turn might lead to war. The Van Buren administration declined, and Texas withdrew its offer.

3

Six years later in 1843, U.S. President John Tyler rekindled the fire of Texas annexation, even negotiating an annexation treaty with the Republic. However approval for the treaty failed in the U.S. Congress. It wasn't until two years later that the issue was resolved – the United States Congress passed a resolution to annex the Republic of Texas as a state on February 28, 1845. This resolution was signed by President Tyler. Eight months later, in October, the citizens of Texas voted to approve this annexation, and the Republic of Texas was admitted as the twenty-eighth state in the nation on December 29, 1845.

The government of the Republic transitioned into that of a state, and began to demark some of the larger counties defined after the Texas Revolution into smaller ones. Such was the case with Nacogdoches County, and in April 1846, it was divided into twenty smaller counties: Anderson, Angelina, Camp, Cherokee, Dallas, Delta, Gregg, Henderson, Hopkins, Houston, Hunt, Kaufman, Raines, Rockwall, Rusk, Smith, Trinity, Upshur, Van Zandt, and Wood.

Smith County was named for General James Smith, who came to Texas in 1816 when it was still under Mexican rule, fought in the Texas Revolution, and then served in the Texas-Indian Wars. The State Legislature called for the founding of a county seat, which they voted to be named Tyler, after President John Tyler, to honor him for his work in bringing Texas into the Union.

According to the rules set out for the new counties, a county seat had to be within three miles of the county's geographic center. Local legend holds that the actual center of the county is to the east of present-day Tyler, but the terrain was so bad there that the city was moved to its current location.

A surveying party, led by Thomas Jefferson Hays, surveyed the land later in 1846. One hundred acres were divided into individual lots, and the City of Tyler was born. It was officially incorporated by the Texas State Legislature on

January 29, 1850. The first Smith County Courthouse was a log cabin, but settlers began to arrive, and the city started to grow. By 1851, a Federal Court had been established in Tyler, one of only three in Texas.

With the coming of the Civil War a decade later, a Confederate training camp was established just four miles out of town called Camp Ford. In 1863 it was converted into a prisoner of war camp, the largest one west of the Mississippi. Some 5,400 prisoners came through Camp Ford, and about 327 prisoners died there, giving the camp a mortality rate of 5.9%... one of the lowest of any Civil War prison.

After the War Between the States, the citizens of Tyler got back to their daily lives, and for many people this meant farming... and for the most part, cotton was king. By the 1890s, cotton was the number one crop in the region. In fact, so much cotton was being produced that a surplus occurred, and the prices began to spiral downward.

Postcard showing men harvesting peaches near Tyler, Texas in 1908

5

After the turn of the century, the Federal Agricultural Adjustment Administration began to pay farmers to plant beans, peaches, and other crops instead of cotton.

The city of Tyler continued to grow, and as it did, the citizens began to worry about social matters such as the sale and consumption of alcohol. Fervor arose against the drink, and prohibition was voted into being in Tyler and Smith County in 1901, long before the 18th Amendment made it the law of the land in 1919. Not everyone supported Smith County's prohibition, however, and re-votes periodically came up. On June 5, 1909 a vote upheld the law, with 2,564 votes for Prohibition, and 1,650 votes against.

A Prohibition Parade on Ferguson Street, from the intersection with North College Avenue, in 1909

As the twentieth century began, something very interesting began to unfold in Tyler. Back in the mid-1800s, a farmer named Matthew Shamburger had begun planting rose bushes along with the peach trees that he was growing in his fields. When a fruit tree blight struck the area, most of that crop was killed. The rose bushes survived, however, giving Shamburger a stream of income. By 1917, Bonnie Shamburger (the grandson of Matthew) was not only selling roses locally, but was shipping rose bushes outside of Texas.

See 20 Million Roses In Bloom, Tyler, Texas

"The Rose Garden of America"

Postcard showing Tyler's rose fields

Other farmers noted this successful crop, and began to grow roses on their own, and by the 1920s many farmers had jumped on the bandwagon of cultivating roses. In a few years the rose business had literally exploded, and it was said that there were periods when a half of the rose bushes produced in the United States were from Tyler and the surrounding area, therefore giving the city the moniker "The Rose Capital of America."

The city embraced the industry. In 1933, an annual Rose Festival was held in the city, organized by the Tyler Garden Club members, local rose growers and the Chamber of Commerce. It continues to this day – a Rose Queen and court are selected, young ladies wear lavish gowns and costumes in the theme of the year's festival, and officiate over the

7

festivities which include a Queen's Tea, a special luncheon, a Coronation ceremony, the Rose Festival Parade, a rose show, an arts and crafts show, an art show, a car show, and even a symphony concert in the park.

A postcard with Rose Queen Dorothy Bell's float in the 1939 Rose Parade

Over the years, Tyler has grown as an industrial capital, becoming a home to many industries, including Tyler Pipe that produces soil and utility pipe products, Trane air conditioners and heat pumps, Carrier Air Conditioners, Cavender's Boot City western wear retailer and manufacturer, and Brookshire's supermarket chain, to name but a few. It has become a progressive city of 260,000 people, and is a hub of commerce in East Texas.

Looking back into the rich history of Tyler, however, there are some locations that seem to have a stronger connection to the city's past than others – in fact, locations where the spirits of days gone by make their presence known. Locations where it is not unusual for a spectral figure to be seen walking the old hallways... where sights, scents and sounds reflect visitors from a bygone era... where the people of today have become witness to the supernatural side of the city's past.

When night falls on the rose bushes, the spirits of Tyler, seem to come alive.

Join us in visiting these wonderful old locations looking for the spirits of Tyler and its surrounding area as we explore the haunts of days long past. Welcome to the ghostly side of Tyler, Texas.

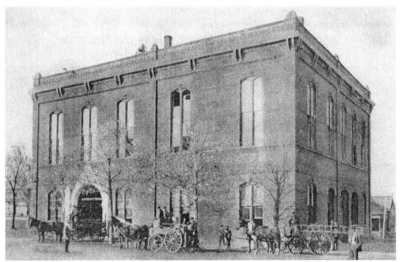

The 1886 Central Fire Station

The Haunted Fire Station

Central Fire Station, Tyler

While one might expect old family homes, hospitals, or even a graveyard or two to be haunted, not many folks would imagine that a fire house would have a ghost – yet the old Central Fire Station is said to have had one very special resident spirit.

The building was erected in 1886 at the corner of College and Locust Streets, a two-story structure that served not only the fire department, but as city hall and the police department as well. Local legend has it that the building appeared in *Ripley's Believe it or Not* newspaper column because at forty feet high, it was the world's tallest two-story building – high enough for four stories.

Prior to that, Tyler was served only by a volunteer fire department. One of the earliest members, and a driving force behind fire protection in the city, was a man named Joe

11

Daglish. He was a railroad employee who took an interest in firefighting, and organized a "bucket brigade" early on.

A firefighting bucket brigade

Because of his efforts, an organized fire department slowly arose out of group of loosely-affiliated citizens, and soon Tyler had a group of full-time firefighters, and their equipment and facilities included a gasoline fire engine, a Bishop and Babcock chemical wagon, and two fire stations in town. Joe Daglish – or "Uncle Joe" as he was known – was made Fire Chief because of his efforts.

Uncle Joe was a bachelor, and he lived in the upstairs quarters of the fire station so that he'd never be very far away from the job, although he did run for mayor of Tyler in 1915 and won. As the head of the city, he continued to grow the fire department with both staff and equipment.

The Tyler Fire Department's Bishop and Babcock chemical wagon

A personal tragedy struck when he developed diabetes, a disease that quickly ravaged his body. He had to have both legs amputated, and was confined to a wheelchair for the rest of his life. Instead of moving to a nursing facility or out of town with one of his relatives, Uncle Joe chose to remain at the fire station. He was allowed to live there and the fireman took care of him just as they would a family member.

Uncle Joe remained active – even though he could no longer serve as a fireman or go out on calls, he carefully studied the daily reports and gave his opinions on the department's activities. He spent the rest of his day playing dominoes with the firemen, or visiting with friends who came by to see him. Although the fire station was not wheelchair-accessible, the firemen would gladly carry his chair up and down the stairs as needed – he was their friend, and they all loved him, as did the city. Joe always had a smile on his face, which was covered by his white beard that matched the hair on his head. His blue eyes that were framed by wire-rimmed glasses seemed to always be laughing.

The Tyler Fire Department fighting a blaze in the 1930s

It was a sad day for the Tyler Fire Department on November 27, 1935, when Uncle Joe passed away. He was given a hero's burial, but the men in the Fire Department weren't convinced that Joe was ready to move on. As long as the Central Fire Station stood, people reported hearing the footsteps of Uncle Joe Daglish, his legs restored, pacing back and forth on the wooden floor of the living quarters upstairs when no living person was up there.

His voice was often heard as well, shouting commands to the firefighters as he had done when he first organized the department. Uncle Joe was still a part of their lives, and the men loved it.

The Central Fire Station was torn down in 1955, and today in its place is a bank and parking lot. The spirit of Uncle Joe may have finally moved on, at rest, his days of fighting Tyler's fires over.

The site of the fire station today – a parking lot

The Fire Station was located at the corner
of College and Locust Streets, Tyler

Disembodied Footsteps, Rising Mist, & a Smoking Ghost!

The Wood-Verner Cemetery, Tyler

As graveyards go, the Wood-Verner Cemetery in the small community known as Black Fork, a suburb of Tyler, Texas, is a very peaceful one. It was originally a parcel of land owned by John Lollar. Mr. Lollar was a local businessman who wanted to see the area grow. He bought up huge tracks of land all over the Tyler area and encouraged other businessmen to build there, which helped the community to flourish. Interestingly enough, John Lollar is most remembered today, not as a founding father of the Smith County region, but as the man who gave us two of its oldest cemeteries.

In 1849, he sold several acres near the heart of Tyler to John Madison Patterson. In the deed, it was stipulated that five

17

acres of this land was to be set aside for a "burying ground." This designated burying spot eventually became the historic Oakwood Cemetery and was first used as such in 1852. Realizing that there would always be a need for a place for folks to lay their loved ones to rest, he also deeded a smaller property about fifteen mites west from the center of town to the Black Fork Methodist Episcopal Church in 1855.

This property became known as the Black Fork Cemetery. Before its official designation, its first resident, Mr. John Gordon, had already been interred there in 1850, making it one of the oldest known graveyards in the Dixie area. As more people moved to Smith County, there were more deceased being laid to rest there, including pioneers, Polish immigrants, slaves, and Civil War veterans. As time passed, the name changed to the Verner Cemetery, and then to the present Wood-Verner Cemetery, thusly titled after two prominent families who owned surrounding land at that time.

Most of the graves date from the mid-1800s into the 1940s, with very few coming later. Unfortunately there are also some unmarked graves, and some markers that have been so worn by time that they are unreadable. Including the unmarked and unreadable stone grates, there are 177 people buried in Wood-Verner.

Sadly, the railroad tracks and major highways have by-passed the community of Black Fork. Because of this, most businesses and residents moved to the thriving city of Tyler and left Black Fork to become the almost-forgotten memory that it is today.

Some folks from the area will tell you the spirits of Wood-Verner Cemetery don't always rest easy. Because of its secluded nature, and due to the fact that it is in a cul-de-sac with a road leading solely to and around it, young people have used it as a sort of lovers lane for years. One couple in particular recounted an event that occurred when they were parked there one moonlit night in the 1960s. They said they had some light tunes playing on the radio and were kissing quite passionately, when they heard what sounded like a gunshot coming from the gated cemetery. They turned to look and saw a man dressed in what appeared to be Civil War military attire walking toward them. He aimed his rifle at them and before the startled couple could even duck, he disappeared. Of course, they didn't hang around to see if he would come back.

Years later, in the 1980s, a young man was waiting on his lady friend to join him there one night. He had exited his car and was walking through the grates, killing time until she could meet him. He got to a certain point and thought he heard someone walking behind him. He turned quickly, but no one was there. Writing it off as his imagination, he kept on meandering through the cemetery. Every few feet he would hear the crunch of grass behind him as if someone was following him... yet each time he turned, there was no one there. He became a little frightened, so he headed back toward his car and quickened his pace. The steps behind him quickened as well, in time with his. Before the young man knew it, he was in an all-out run and was sure something was going to tackle him at any moment. He made it back to his car and never saw a thing. Since then, it has been said that if you walk in the cemetery at night, it is possible that someone – or something – will walk behind you and you might even hear their footsteps.

A sheriff's deputy, who is a friend of mine, told me that he used to go up to this cemetery at night and sit in his patrol car to get some of his paperwork done undisturbed and also to discourage teenagers from parking there. He said one night in 2012 he was sitting there with his nose buried in his papers when he heard something knocking on the passenger side of his car. It gave him quite a start and he couldn't see anybody through the window. He laughed it off as his imagination and went back to his work. A few minutes later he heard a strange weeping sound coming from the cemetery and when he turned to look, "something that looked like a bright white mist rose out of the ground" about three feet from his window and flew over his car. He immediately left and refuses to go sit there anymore. He says he does not believe in ghosts, but he has no explanation for what he saw – he believes that sometimes it's just best to leave well enough alone.

Having heard these stories, I knew this was a site I had to check out. On my first venture to find the cemetery, I got lost. The directions the officer gave me were hard to follow and involved a few oil roads and I guess I turned left when I should have turned right. I did not give up and resorted to using my GPS on my phone. That didn't quite work either, as it left me high and dry at an intersection of the new Hwy 49 that was being built there at the time. I eventually drove on past where the GPS stopped and used some of the clues the officer had given me to find it.

There is absolutely no reason to go down the little oil road that leads to Wood-Verner unless your destination is the graveyard, because that is all you will find. No one lives there, and there isn't anything but trees on either side whose branches meet at the top causing a cave effect over the road. Still, it wasn't exactly creepy... it just had the feeling of age and seclusion.

It was dusk when I drove in and the first thing I noticed as I pulled up to the gates was the historical marker placed just inside, designating it as the oldest known graveyard in the Dixie area. I read the sign and felt a strange sense of sadness wash over me. Having lived in the East Texas region most of my life and only having just now discovered that this place existed, I wondered how many people were aware it was there. It seemed sad and lonely out in the woods by itself, and yet it was serene and quiet as well. I became aware that it was almost too quiet. There were no birds chirping and there was no wind blowing. The only sound to be heard was that of the occasional traffic coming from the new highway hundreds of yards away.

I had taken a friend with me and she said it felt like we were being watched. I didn't get that sensation but as we entered the cemetery itself, the feeling of sadness deepened with every step. I also felt a strong desire to clean up some of the weed-covered graves and tried to do so where I could.

I spoke out loud as we walked through. I asked if anyone was with us, and for them to let us know if they were. I introduced myself and my friend and said that we meant no harm. I repeated the stories I had heard about the place and at one point both myself and my friend did hear what sounded like the crunching of footsteps on grass behind us.

Not being of a timid nature, I pressed on until we were in the back corner of the graveyard. We stopped there and examined a grave from the 1800s that was off by itself. A doctor was buried there; it seemed odd that he was buried alone. The feeling of sadness was intense at that point and we decided it was time to leave.

As we walked back toward the front gates I took out a cigarette and announced out loud my apologies if my smoking bothered anyone buried there. At that moment I felt a cold sensation in my hand as if something was trying to take the cigarette from me. I told my friend what was happening as we stopped near some grates on the side of the lot and I held out my hand with the palm up and placed the cigarette upon it. I asked out loud if there was a smoker buried there and told them they could have the cigarette if they could take it from my hand. Incredibly, in a matter of seconds the cold sensation intensified and the cigarette began to rock back and forth and then leapt out of my hand and fell to the ground. My friend gasped in disbelief and asked me to try it again.

I made mention of the fact that there was no wind blowing and that I had held my hand still and flat. She agreed and encouraged me to light the cigarette this time. I did so and again placed it in my hand, this time with the lit end extended out a bit off my hand. I asked out loud for someone to take the cigarette again and offered them a smoke as I held it there for them. As I said this, the lit end of the cigarette, or cherry as it is called, flared up as if someone was indeed taking a puff and the smoke increased as if they were exhaling. The cold sensation was back and I felt the cigarette begin to move.

I asked aloud for them to take it from my hand and agreed to leave it there for them on a grave if they could do it. My friend's mouth hung open in disbelief as it did slowly move then jump out of my hand.

I picked it up and placed it carefully on the top of a gravestone so that it wouldn't burn anything and we walked away. I announced it was their cigarette now, that they had earned it.

The cigarette on the headstone

As we walked away, we kept turning back to watch what was happening, and the cigarette kept burning and smoking. The manufacturers put breaks in the cigarettes these days to cause them to go out if you aren't puffing on them. It is a safety precaution in case someone was to drop one unnoticed or fall asleep with one. But this one went right on smoking through those breaks.

We went back out through the gates and decided to walk around the exterior just to see what we could and when we reached the side where we had left the cigarette, I saw that it was smoked to the butt and out. We took a few pictures of the grave it was sitting on and of the cemetery in general and headed back to the car.

Is Wood-Verner haunted? I can't explain what happened that day without saying yes. If you decide to check it out for yourself, please remember it is a spiritual place and should be treated with respect.

To find Wood-Verner Cemetery, take Hwy 64 west from Tyler to the intersection of FM 724 and turn right (northwest). Go to intersection of CR1148 and turn left (west). Continue to the end of CR1148. The road ends at and circles the cemetery.

Haunted Dining at
Gilbert's El Charro 1

Local folks might argue that Gilbert's El Charro restaurant is the best Tex-Mex food this side of the Mississippi. Having eaten there a time or two myself, I would venture to say they have a pretty good argument. And whether you agree or not, both El Charro locations have been a Tyler tradition for over seventy years. It has gotten to where people don't go there just to eat anymore. They go there because they know their friends will be there. They know their neighbors will be there. They know every lunch or dinner is like sitting down at your home table without the work or mess. Three generations have gone there to eat and socialize. It has lasted for seventy years and shows no signs of slowing down.

The founder of the restaurant, Gilberto Ramirez, immigrated to the United States from Mexico when he was only sixteen years old. He arrived without money or means but he had the determination to make a success of himself. He began working in a restaurant and quickly earned a reputation as a hard worker and a fast learner. In 1943, he moved to Tyler, found a good location, and opened his own restaurant. He dubbed this new eatery "El Charro."

A "charro" was actually a derogatory term for a Mexican Cowboy who adorned himself with lots of shiny bangles and threads. "Real" cowboys thought they were a joke and called them "sissies." But through time they proved to be a tough breed and handled themselves on the range as well as any rough and ready cowpoke. Eventually the charro gained respect and became sort of a legend of the West.

Perhaps Mr. Ramirez identified with the story of the charro as a character in whom people had little faith but who managed to rise above it all in his own stylish way to become an icon. Whatever the case, the formula worked, and the first location eventually spawned a second a few miles up the road. Today the third generation of the Ramirez family runs the business and if you are ever in the Tyler area, I encourage you to stop in and say hello to Manny at El Charro 1, or Rosa at El Charro 2. Have a margarita and be sure to try their award-winning chicken fried steak platter!

I had just finished attending a business expo where I had been promoting my business when I got a call from a lady saying her business was haunted and she wanted to speak with me discreetly. As the conversation progressed I discovered I was talking to Rosa, the current owner/manager of the establishment. She and her brother had been experiencing things in the restaurants for years and she had been too intimidated by the weirdness of it to tell anyone or ask for help. When she saw me at the expo and learned what I did, she decided to take a chance and ask me to come hear her story.

I arrived at El Charro 1 the following Saturday with a small team of investigators and met Rosa face to face. As we sat and talked she told me that the employees had reported glasses moving at the bar when no one was around. She told me they often heard voices and strange noises that could not be accounted for. More than one employee had heard a female crying in the ladies room, but not a living soul was in there when they went to investigate. My mouth hung open when she went on to relate the story of one of her female employees levitating a foot off the ground right in front of her. She said the girl was so shaken up she almost went into hysterics.

I asked her if she had any idea what might have caused the establishment to become such a spiritually active place. She told me a story that haunts me to this day. Glenda Moorehead, the head waitress of the place in 1988 had left from there one

27

day after work and disappeared. Her car was found the next morning in the parking lot of a local bar with the keys in the ignition, her purse with all its contents sitting in the seat. A trail of blood led to the back door of the bar and her shoe was found at the side, but Glenda had vanished without a trace and had never been heard from again. This is still an unsolved crime in Tyler and Rosa believes that Glenda's spirit had come back to a place she knew well and where she was loved... Gilbert's El Charro 1.

Rosa told us how everyone loved Glenda and how she used to hang out after her shift ended and have a margarita and play the Pac-Man arcade game that used to sit in the corner. She told me she had looked up to Glenda like a big sister and how she still missed her. She thought the woman crying in the ladies room might be her, as that room was located near her favorite spot where the arcade game used to be. Evidently a few customers had even been waited on by her, because when their living waitress came to take their order they said they had already given it to a lady matching Glenda's description, though there was no one working at the time that matched that appearance.

Rosa went on to say that she felt like her father was there, too and possibly one of the long-time cooks that had passed away after years of dedicated service. Sometimes, she said, she felt as if her father was watching them and helping them to carry on. Her brother, Manny, echoed these remarks and said he had seen things move and heard strange things himself that he could not explain. Both agreed there was more going on than could be rationalized by logic.

We conducted an investigation of the restaurant that night. We had all of our equipment set up, and we were prepared for anything. The night started slowly with a few bumps here and there and an orb or two showing up on camera. But before we packed it in, we had gotten much more than we thought we would. One of our party was touched and the camera happened to catch a swirling light fly away from her as she reacted. Another of our group heard a man's voice whispering to her. The temperature dropped drastically in one area of the storage room just as I was pinched in the side. But the most startling piece of evidence we gathered came at around 3:30AM. The camera caught the lid of a big storage can full of dry pinto beans rise up and go down in the can while no one was near. We had absolutely no explanation for it.

I have no doubt someone haunts El Charro 1 in Tyler, Texas, but I can't prove who it is. Is it the father watching over his business and his descendants? Could it be the old cook still making sure things are prepared as he likes them to be? Or is the spirit of the head waitress hanging out in the place she knew so well? Who can say? But if you ever go there and your waitress disappears before you get your order, it's definitely not bad service, it may just mean you have been visited by one of the restaurant's spirits.

El Charro 1 is located at 2604 E. Erwin Street in Tyler, Texas.

Spooky Seconds at El Charro 2

If the haunts of El Charro 1 are not to your liking, give the ones at El Charro 2 a try. Just a few miles up the road from the original location, El Charro 2 was opened in a large old house on the corner of a busy intersection in the early 1960s. It was an immediate success due to all the overflow of customers from number one. Folks came from miles around to try out the new location and the Ramirez family was very happy to treat them to the same hospitality they had doled out in generous helpings at the original restaurant.

While this location has a more modern style, it definitely stayed true to the vision of Mr. Gilbert Ramirez, the founding father. The atmosphere is more like a traditional Tex-Mex eatery with an old world flavor. Of course, with the opening of a second location, came double the staff, double the customers and double the headaches.

In 1997, it caught fire and burned to the ground. No one knows for sure why or how the fire started but it certainly destroyed every bit of the restaurant. The theory is that it began as a grease fire in the kitchen. Luckily no one died in the blaze. Perhaps it is what happened next that caused this location to be inhabited by entities from the other side.

The clientele demanded it be re-built and the family agreed it should be. So, interestingly enough, they pushed all the burned debris, including the old grill and kitchen fixtures, into what was the basement of the house and covered it over with dirt. They then built the new restaurant right on top of the ashes of the old. Maybe this seemed like a good idea at the time, but some say it was bad karma and caused the new building itself to forever remain unsettled.

Customers and employees alike began complaining of strange voices that could not be identified calling their names. Pots and pans moved about the kitchen of their own accord. And a little girl has been seen running and playing and suddenly disappearing in the lobby. Employees have attributed tugs on their clothing and touches on their arms to this little girl looking for attention. No one has a clue who she is or how she came to reside there.

At the request of Rosa, the Owner/Manager, I spent the night in the building with a few of my fellow ghost hunters. We heard many unexplained noises throughout the night and captured a few interesting pictures with anomalies in them. But there was one thing that happened that made me a believer in the spirits that reside there.

Near the front entrance, there is a long wooden bench. Beside that bench, there is a solid metal rocking chair. We were taking a break from searching for evidence and I had walked to the front to have a seat and look over some of the pictures I had been taking. As I neared the counter, I looked over and saw that the rocking chair was in full rock with no one anywhere near it.

I yelled for the rest of the group to get up there and record this immediately. The investigator with the video recorder did manage to get there in time to record several minutes of the chair rocking. We stood in awe of the spectacle until someone started taking pictures and talking to the chair. We asked if anyone was there and if they would allow us to take their picture. The chair began to slow as our cameras all began to flash and I was sure we had frightened whatever was there with us away.

After we watched the chair come to a complete stop, we began analyzing the pictures we had taken. Out of all the hundreds we snapped in that short amount of time, only two held anything of interest. The first had a ray of light moving out of the chair. The second had a ball of light moving away from the chair and over the wooden bench and when we zoomed in to view it closer, it was very clear that there was a little girl's face in it. It was definitely an "oh crap!" moment. None of us could believe it.

One of the investigators sitting in the rocking chair

Nothing else happened inside the restaurant that night and so we decided to pack up our things and head for home. I had just finished putting my things in my bag and walked outside at about five in the morning. It was still very dark out and traffic had just barely begun to pick up at the start of the new day. I stood out in front of the building under the awning, near the newspaper racks, and contemplated what we had seen. For some reason, I felt compelled to verbalize a thank you to the little girl spirit that had shown herself to us that night. I said out loud: "Thank you, little girl, for allowing us to see that. We mean you no harm and we really appreciate you doing that for us." Immediately as I uttered the last word, my bag was jerked from my hand and hit the ground and the newspaper stand near me flew open.

There was no wind. I can't explain it. I know what I saw and what I felt. I would like to think she was telling me she heard me and she was playing with me a little bit, but she could have just as easily been telling me to leave her alone. I don't know. But I do know she chose the one moment I was completely alone with no equipment out to do this.

So if you decide to partake of the excellent food at El Charro 2 and you feel a tug on your sleeve, or see a large metal rocking chair rocking by itself, pay it no mind, it's just the little spirit that lives there. Tell her hello for me and try not to stare. I don't think she likes it.

El Charro 2 is located in Tyler, Texas at 2623 East Fifth Street, at the intersection of Fifth Street and Loop 323.

A UFO photographed downtown?!? Well, no, this is just a mock-up. No such pictures have been taken... at least... not yet!

UFOs Over Tyler

While this chapter isn't about ghosts, it certainly falls in the category of outside-the-normal. In the 1950s, a wave of UFO mania swept across the nation. Unidentified Flying Objects, also dubbed "flying saucers," were being spotted in most every state, and Texas was not exempt from the phenomena.

The "flying saucer" moniker accepted by most people as originating in 1947, when pilot Kenneth Arnold made the first reported Unidentified Flying Object sighting in the United States. He was searching for a missing airplane over the Mt. Ranier, Washington area, when he saw nine unusual objects flying in a chain on June 24, 1947. He described them to a reporter by saying, "They flew erratic, like a saucer if you skip it across the water." In his article for the newspaper, the reporter wrote of Kenneth Arnold, "He said he sighted nine saucer-like aircraft flying in formation..." And so, as the story goes, the term "flying saucer" was born.

In reality, the description of a UFO as a saucer was first used several decades earlier just a couple of hours northwest of Tyler in Dennison, Texas. A farmer named John Martin was hunting on January 2, 1878, when he saw a round object fly over his head. This was years before the Wright brothers would make their famous flight at Kitty Hawk, so the sighting was a startling event. He reported it to the authorities, and on January 25, 1878 the *Denison Daily News* ran a story with the headline *A Strange Phenomenon*:

"From Mr. John Martin, a farmer who lives some six miles south of this city, we learn the following strange story: Tuesday morning while out hunting, his attention was directed to a dark object high up in the southern sky. The peculiar shape and velocity with which the object seemed to approach riveted his attention and he strained his eyes to discover its character."

"When first noticed, it appeared to be about the size of an orange, which continued to grow in size. After gazing at it for some time Mr. Martin became blind from long looking and left off viewing it for a time in order to rest his eyes. On resuming his view, the object was almost overhead and had increased considerably in size, and appeared to be going through space at wonderful speed."

"When directly over him it was about the size of a large saucer and was evidently at great height. Mr. Martin thought it resembled, as well as he could judge, a balloon. It went as rapidly as it had come and was soon lost to sight in the heavenly skies. Mr. Martin is a gentleman of undoubted veracity and this strange occurrence, if it was not a balloon, deserves the attention of our scientists."

Texas never did get its due credit for the saucer description, but as the years went by the Lone Star State has been the site of many UFO sightings. From the Aurora airship in 1897, to the Stephenville lights in 2008, to more recent sightings that continue to be reported, Texas has always been a hotbed of UFO activity.

Many of the sightings over the years have been in the Pineywoods area of the state, including Tyler and Smith County, as you'll see from the following accounts.

April 1975 – A young man traveling along a highway outside of Tyler saw a bright light in his rearview mirror. It soon began to overtake him, and soon his car was illuminated as it paced him from above. Even stranger than the light itself was the fact that the craft made absolutely no sound. In a few minutes, it pulled slightly ahead of the car, and then suddenly sped off into the darkness of the night.

April 1981 – A woman was driving home to Tyler from the Metroplex on I-20, when she saw an object glowing orange in the sky. She thought that the setting sun might be glinting off of the wing of an airplane, until she saw that not only was it lower than an airplane would be, but it also seemed to be following her. As darkness fell the orange light appeared brighter. When she finally exited toward Tyler, she was relieved to see that the craft – whatever it was – continued along I-20.

March 1986 – Two people were driving along a country road in Smith County, when a craft appeared in the darkness above them. It was large, disc-shaped, and was glowing with an orange light. The bottom of the object was dark. There seemed to be an energy emanating from the ship that seemed to be affecting their car. Terrified, the driver pushed the gas pedal to the floor and sped away, never looking back.

December 1988 – A gentleman driving into Tyler one evening spotted a bright light in the sky coming toward him. Thinking that it might be a helicopter, he stopped his car to watch it. As it passed over his head, he saw that it was a circular object with a reddish-glow. As low as the large object was flying, there should have been some type of noise – rotors from a helicopter or the engines from a plane, yet the night was silent as it passed.

August 2006 – A Tyler couple were outside on a very cloudy night – the moon and stars were all obscured by the cloud cover. A light caught their attention, and they watched as a light hovered beneath the clouds for some time. It seemed to be changing colors from white, to blue, to red, and then back to white again. There was no explanation for the object. As suddenly as it had appeared, it vanished into the night.

January 2008 – Two hunters saw a bright light in the sky that was stationary at first, but suddenly took off at a high rate of speed. It disappeared into the night, leaving the hunters wondering what had just happened. When they returned home, they were ridiculed for their UFO story, until reports on the news indicated that others had seen the same thing that night.

November 2009 – a couple walked outside early one morning to see a shiny object moving irregularly in the sky. It was darting about like no airplane could do, and even appeared to be changing colors at times. They watched it for several minutes before it finally disappeared.

January 2012 – a Tyler resident saw a bright object streaking above the downtown area. It was traveling fast, with a blinking light and an orange light just behind it. When he began talking about it, explanations were offered such as it being a flashing light on a tower of some sort, but none could account for the movement – and appearance – of the object.

February 2012 – A family was out walking one evening when they saw a bright, orange ball of light moving toward them above the tree-line. It seemed to hover above them for a time, moving about as if it had conscious control of its movements. When they began to run toward their home, it disappeared. Looking back, they knew that it was definitely not a helicopter or airplane, but they could come up with no rational explanation for it.

The stories and sightings go on and on: A flashing object hovering in the southern Smith County sky in 1999, golden "orbs" flying from southeast to northwest over Tyler in 2009, a reddish-orange ball moving over the city at a steady speed in 2010, and many, many more.

The reports have some consistencies – bright lights, often reddish or orange in color, moving intelligently in the sky unlike an airplane or helicopter would, without any sound at all.

As I was researching the stories for this chapter, one of the most intriguing reports came from a gentleman that I interviewed. Like most everyone else, he did not want his name mentioned, and understandably so – whether you're talking about ghosts, UFOs, or monsters in the night, people tend to look at you a little differently when you take a stand that the unreal, the unthinkable, the supernatural is actually quite real.

He was kind enough to share his story with me, though. He was out in his yard one evening under the stars of an East Texas night. One star in the distance appeared to be moving, so he watched as it came toward him, growing larger and larger. In only a few moments, the bright ball of light flew over his head and disappeared into the distance. As bright as it was, the object made absolutely no sound.

I asked, "Could it have been a low-flying airplane?"

He shook his head, and said, "It was a ball of light, not a plane."

"How about a helicopter?" I mused.

"Moved too fast. And there wasn't any sound. Nothing at all," he said somberly.

That had pretty much ruled out most man-made things, so I finally asked, "So what do you think that it was?"

I'll never forget his reply.

He looked at me evenly, without emotion, and said, "Don't know." He paused a minute, and then added, "I try not to think about it too much."

41

There's something about his eyes that let me know he had been thinking about it, at least, more than he let on. And his account was eerily similar to that farmer who reported the object flying over his head in 1878.

To make this topic even more interesting, I also had my own encounter with an unknown flying object on the Cherokee Trace, which I'll be sharing with you in just a few chapters.

What is going on in the skies over Tyler and Smith County? Only time will tell, as the reports continue to come in about the red/orange lights flying along without making a sound, showing themselves to the residents as if to silently say, "We're here..."

The House on McDonald Road

A Private Home in Tyler

I often get calls from people who have heard about my interest in ghosts and the supernatural. I usually try to get a good feel for the person through phone conversation before I commit to doing an investigation or even offering advice. There are quite a few eccentrics out there who just want attention or just want to feel special by claiming their house is haunted. I have gotten pretty good at discerning what is worth checking into and what is not.

One afternoon I got a call from a fellow who told me he was living in a haunted house. At first, he sounded a bit confused as to what he should and shouldn't tell me. I was just about to write him off and tell him I was busy when he began to tell me the story of his mother. She had passed away just a couple years ago, he said, and he firmly believed she had not only come back to tell him goodbye, but that she had come back several times and had brought other spirits with her.

I asked him to tell me about his house and why he thought he was being haunted. He told me his home was nothing special. He said it was just your average middle-class, one story, three bedroom home in an average neighborhood. The house was built in the 1970s and was near U.T. Tyler. He stated that he had lived there for eight years prior to the haunting starting and it had taken the last two years to get up the nerve to tell someone about it. It all began a few hours after his mother had passed away, he said.

I pressed him to tell me exactly what had happened and I turned on my recorder to make sure I got it all. I wanted to be able to listen to it again on my own and decide if I should head over to his house or not. I also wanted to make sure he didn't change his story on me later, as I have had happen before.

This is almost word for word what he said:

"I had driven around crying and thinking for a while after my mother passed away at the hospital. I didn't want to face anyone and I didn't really know what to do. Eventually I realized I needed to go home because my eight-year-old daughter was there with the babysitter (my wife had divorced me a few months prior) and I knew she would be worried. When I arrived at my house, I told my daughter that her grandmother had passed away. We both cried for a long time and decided to go to bed early and try to not think about it anymore.

"I let her come lay in the bed with me to comfort her as much as I could. We talked and cried some more and eventually she went to sleep but I could not. I lay there staring at the ceiling and asking the usual question of why this had to happen when something around me changed.

"There was wind in my room. It was strong and grew stronger to what seemed like a cyclone force. There was a tapping, almost a drumming on the bed beside me. I heard my daughter say 'Nanny!' (her word for my mother) excitedly… and yet when I looked, my daughter was asleep.

"I turned over and propped myself up and my mother was laying on the other side of my daughter in the bed. She raised up and leaned over her and towards me. I could hear the wind blowing…making a 'whooshing' sound.

"'See, I came to see you,' my mother said in a reassuring motherly kind of way.

"I called out 'Mom, where are you?' and she replied that it was hard to explain, but she was okay. Her face was wavering with spikey light and the wind was blowing her hair. It was like she was having difficulty… like she was under attack. But even though she appeared to be having this difficulty, there were moments when she seemed to come together and have clarity.

"I asked her to come back to me. Her face got solemn and she said 'Honey, I can't,' and then more intensely, 'and I don't want to.' It was if she was pleading with me to understand.

"I told her, 'But Mom, I love you and I miss you.' The wind began to get louder and stronger. She said, 'I know (and here she was almost crying), but son you have to understand… I am THE LIVING REIN OF THE ONE GOD.' At this point my mind was almost slammed back with a strong image that I felt like was incredibly important to remember.

"I saw warm, magnificent, radiant rays of light. And through the light I saw a herd of thousands of horses stampeding across a big dark sandy area with dark mountains in the background. Dust was being kicked up in billowing clouds that obscured many of the horses. Each horse had a single rein that seemed to come from a place on the back of its neck and stretch back to a huge hand that was high above and behind them. The hand belonged to a big, beautiful, masculine figure in a chariot. I could not see his face or really any more than a vague outline, but the hand was very clear, and the light was incredible. I got the impression Mom was referring to the reins on the horses as being alive and she was one of them. The

45

rein nearest me began to glow... and the stallion it was attached to became very clear. It was struggling against the rein and charging forward. Somehow, I felt like that horse might be me.

"It had become much harder for her to talk and to maintain her form. The wind got even louder and I wondered why my daughter did not wake up. Mom looked at me with intense eyes. She wanted to say more, and it was as if she was pleading with me to understand. Then she laid her head back and her mouth opened very wide. The spikey light that surrounded her got brighter and then she was gone.

"I snapped out of it and noticed my legs felt warm, like something was on them and then I felt two taps on the pillow beside me again. 'THE LIVING REIN OF THE ONE GOD' came out of my mouth and I knew I must get up and write it all down immediately because I was meant to remember this and I was meant to share it.

"I wish I could have talked with my mother more. I miss her so much."

When he was done I kindly thanked him for calling and took down his contact information. I was more than a little blown away by what he had told me. He had gone on to say that he had hired a local artist to paint the image that had been burned into his mind and he had it hanging in his dining room. He also said that strange things he could not explain had been happening since then including things flying off shelves, pictures falling off walls, disembodied voices, footsteps entering a room when no one was there, and shadows that appeared and disappeared for no reason.

Clearly, he believed something was in his house besides the living. He even confessed to trying to "cleanse" the house with white sage but he used the words "all negative or evil entities must leave with the spoke but all positive entities are welcome" because he could not bear the thought of driving his mother away if, indeed, she was there. It occurred to me that by using that choice of words, he may have just invited lots of new guests into his home and that the definition of "positive" did not rule out pranksters and lonely spirits who just want attention.

The Vision painting

After listening to the recording of the phone conversation a few times, I decided I would meet with the man. I still was not one hundred percent he was experiencing a haunting, or if he was just allowing his deep-seated grief to manifest. It seemed possible that he was literally wishing his mother back into his life in the only way he could... in spirit. However, he seemed earnest enough and my gut told me to give it a shot. This being the case, I rounded up a couple of the ghost hunting gang, set up an appointment, and headed to his home.

We arrived at the modest, unassuming house at around 8PM and after receiving a warm welcome, he showed us around the place. As he had described it was just an average middle class home that he shared with his daughter and his sister. He showed us the picture he had had painted of his experience after his mother passed and it was very nicely done.

When the short tour was over, he explained he had sent his daughter and sister to stay with a friend for the night and told us we had free run of the home.

We spent the entire night there and we were surprised at how much evidence we captured. Almost immediately we all agreed there was a strong sense of being watched... and disapprovingly, at that. We then caught two distinct human-shaped shadows moving on our DVR system when no one was near. Next we captured one EVP of a woman saying "Why are you here?" and she added the name of one of our party to the query. But the most interesting thing that happened was our things were rearranged in our large case that we carry our equipment in.

We were in another part of the house trying to get a response on our recorders when we heard a rattling noise coming from the master bedroom. This happened to be where we had left our case, so we hurriedly returned to see if something was wrong with our equipment. We came in the room in time to see the camera strap still swinging on the camera that was now lying beside the case on a chair. The cord had been wrapped around the leg of the chair several times. The things in the case were jumbled up as if someone had been rummaging through it. None of us were in the room when this happened and all the doors were locked from the inside. I think someone or some spirit got curious to see what all we had in the case.

The homeowner verified that all these things were similar to what happened to him on a daily basis. He asked us if he needed to be worried. I told him none of us detected anything that we felt was evil, but we understood how the incidents could be annoying or even frightening. I offered him the phone number of a very good psychic I knew and told him if he wanted to rid himself of the haunting, this was the person to call.

When morning came, we thanked him for the opportunity to experience these things first hand and told him we were leaving the next step in his hands. He could either go on living with it or call the psychic and try to resolve it. He smiled at us and said that as long as there was no evil or malice in it, he didn't mind sharing his home with spirits. Then he thanked us for coming and invited us back any time.

When I decided to write this book, I called him to get permission to put this segment in and to check on how things were going. He said mysterious things had continued to happen but nothing had really bothered him or his daughter. He had gotten involved in a new and more healthy relationship with a beautiful lady and was happy. Evidently the lady that now lived with them had also begun to experience the phenomena and was more than a little amused by it. She fit right in. He gave me permission to write about his home and invited me back again.

I enjoyed my night of investigating on McDonald Road and think I even managed to make a new friend out of it. One thing is certain – there is more than meets the eye going on there, and all of it seems welcomed by the tenants. Maybe the living and the dead can acknowledge each other and manage to live together in peace.

The home is located at an address I can't disclose on McDonald Road in Tyler. The homeowner asks that his privacy be respected, and that he have no unexpected ghost hunters or paranormal enthusiasts show up unannounced. However, if you happen to be in the area and see him in the yard, he will be glad to tell you about his experiences in the house.

The Real Terror of Terror Nights

Terror Nights Haunted Attraction, Tyler, Texas

On the South side of Tyler, near the railroad tracks, in a series of warehouses that look like something out of your nightmares, sits the number one haunted attraction in East Texas. It is known as Terror Nights Haunted House and it has been delivering tours into horror for six years now. Every Halloween people come from a hundred mile radius to pay their money, stand in line, and experience the frightening fun put on by the actors in this made-up haunt. I wonder how many of the folks who come realize that the building is really haunted?

Terror Nights is the brain child of brothers Jeff and Ryan Laepple. It began in 2008 as one big pay-for-scares Halloween attraction and has since grown into two frightening attractions in one location. Killer clowns, psychotic escaped patients, werewolves, and yes, even deranged bunny rabbits, played by local actors, do their best to evoke screams from everyone who goes through. More than one 'smack talker' has left running, afraid to look and see what might be chasing them. Every year, more folks come to enjoy it and every year it gets bigger and better.

Ryan and Jeff are friends of mine and I have visited their place many times. In doing so, I got to know several of the actors who work there. About three years ago, I began to hear stories from the actors about strange things happening behind the scenes. They related stories to me about cold spots and unexplained noises. A couple of them really seemed spooked by the place and voiced concern about ever being there alone.

On a whim, I brought the subject up to Ryan one day and suggested we have an investigation one night. He sort of scoffed at the idea that he might own a REAL haunted house, but he was game to give it a try and a date was set. I had no idea if we would be wasting our time or not, but I thought it would be pretty cool to be alone in a haunted attraction over night. With this thought in mind, I infected nine other friends with my excitement.

Ryan was the only one there waiting for us when we arrived at 10PM. It was the off-season but all the haunted effects were still in place. After revving it all up and letting us play for a while during his guided tour of the place we set up a battle plan. It was rather daunting, as the site was even bigger than I realized. In all, he had access to five warehouses on the property and each one was more interesting than the last. One even housed a full scale model of a cave that was used in a horror movie. We divided up, turned off all the lights, and set to work.

When we go on these investigations, we always take walkie-talkies so that we can communicate immediately if something starts to happen. During the second hour, one of my fellow hunters began yelling at me through the walkies to get to where she was as fast as possible. I ran to her location and when I got there I met a near hysterical third member of our group. She was shaking like a leaf and having trouble getting her breath.

They told me they had been in the "clown" area of the haunt when suddenly the temperature began dropping and they had all been overwhelmed with the feeling they were not alone. First they heard footsteps behind them when no one was there, and then one of them felt like she was being attacked or tormented by something. It became hard for her to breathe and she began to shake uncontrollably though she said it had nothing to do with being cold. She felt something touch her and she voiced the need to leave the area – but when she tried to move, she could not. She said her legs were frozen in place and the other two people who were with her literally had to push and pull her to get her moving. At the same time as this was going on with her, their EMF reader had started beeping like mad, indicating something was indeed nearby.

Once she had broken free of whatever invisible force was holding her, they ran all the way back to where I came upon the scene. When we reviewed the footage from the camera later, we found a few interesting things. We did catch the sound of footsteps on the audio. And shortly after that, an orb flew into the lady who then began to shudder. When she was frozen in place, a glowing ball of light flew across in front of her on camera as if it were blocking her way. And we captured and EVP saying "Whoa!" as they tried to leave.

We took a break, caught our breath, and set out again in different groups. This time we used a "ghost box" in the clown area. A ghost box is basically a radio that scans through all the channels of the radio very fast without ever stopping. You can ask questions and supposedly it is easy for a spirit to manipulate the radio to give answers out loud. Sometimes this works very clearly and sometimes not. This was one of the times it definitely worked.

Three other investigators headed to the area where the lady had been affected so strongly. When they arrived, one of them turned on the ghost box and began asking questions. When asked if it could say their names, it replied, "Yes," and actually said one of the hunters' names. When asked if it liked the girl it had messed with earlier it said, "Don't want to talk about her." When asked if it wanted her to come back, it said, "She's a bitch." And when they said they meant it no harm, the box replied, "Don't trust." All this was captured on video and audio. And please keep in mind that this ghost box device scans so fast through the stations that it only manages to grab maybe one word off each channel before it moves on. To get answers as clear as these was outstanding.

While that group was following up in the clown room, myself and two others were going through the "psycho ward" part of the other warehouse. We had several instances where we heard unexplained noises and almost every time the EMF reader went off as if to verify something was there. In addition to the noises, we saw what looked like a shadow man running around a corner, and one of the folks with me felt something touch her on the arm.

It was as if the wind was being generated inside this warehouse.

One of our party members decided to shake the unresponsive lady. She apprehensively eased closer and reached out her hand. As her fingers touched the lady's shoulder, the lady suddenly raised up incredibly fast, causing the helpful hunter to scream. We were all petrified when we looked upon the face of our frozen friend. She had the most insane and scary expression that I have ever seen. She looked as if she could murder us on the spot. The investigator nearest me whispered she was going to douse her with holy water until that murderous look went away.

We all called her name and finally I, along with two others, took her by the arm and started leading her out of there. She protested – she didn't want to leave. I found this incredible, as she had been shivering and near frightened to death just a short time before. We just kept talking to her and pushing and pulling her out of that crazy place. As we got her near the exit, the video camera caught another glowing orb flying away from her. It also caught one flying away from me and though I didn't realize it at the time, the pain in my side stopped at the same moment.

When we left that area and got back to the spot we had originally designated as base, we found Ryan waiting for us. We shared our experiences with him as we packed to go. He was more than a little surprised and agreed that maybe there was something there after all. We thanked him very much for allowing us to investigate, and at 4:30 in the morning, we headed for home.

Later, I compiled the crazy things we captured on video and audio that night and presented it to him as his copy of the evidence. He now shows it on his digital projector for those who are curious about what happened that night. I don't know if he is truly a believer at this point or not, but he seems to take pride in having a truly "haunted" haunted attraction.

I can hardly wait for him to open for this season. I know he has been hard at work changing things up and improving upon it once again. I love going there and I recommend it highly to everyone who reads this. But now I will always wonder if the horrible creature I see in the darkness of Terror Nights is a paid actor, or if I am staring into the face of a spirit. Whether the disfigured clown that jumps out at me is solid or ethereal, the chills that race down my spine are very real.

Terror Nights is located at 816 E. Oakwood Street in Tyler. They are open for business from late September to early November. Visit them online at terrornightshaunt.com

The Crystal Rock Shop

Tyler, Texas

Off the beaten path, in a quiet little neighborhood in South Tyler, there is a shop unlike any other in town. It is known as the Crystal Rock Shop and it sits beside an unassuming home on a residential street. You might even drive right in front of it and never even know it was there. It is definitely a place you would have to seek out, and not one that you might easily stumble across. Yet it has done a tidy little business for many years, and has loyal following of customers that almost look at it as a second home.

The shop deals in every sort of rock, mineral, crystal and ore you can possibly imagine. They also carry incense, herbs, and charms. It began as a labor of love by Mrs. Gean Wheless and her husband Bill in 1985. When they passed away within three weeks of each other in 2004, the shop was passed on to their son, Robert Wheless, who is the current owner. Their adopted (in spirit) daughter, Debi Lacey has been involved in the store for over fifteen years and has managed it for ten.

Gean Wheless was a wonderful woman with the sweetest spirit I have ever heard of. Everyone who came in her shop was immediately family and did not leave without a hug. The folks around Tyler who managed to find her shop, loved her through and through. Many of her customers would come over just to hang out and be around this lively, happy woman. Current store manager, Debi Lacey, was one of those people. She would spend every lunch hour she could with them until one day Gean declared that Debi was her daughter. From that moment on, it became a reality and Debi was literally one of the family.

Debi returned the love she was given by helping with the shop and eventually taking over when Gean and Bill became too feeble to handle it. And though mom and pop Wheless are no longer with us in body, their spirits linger in the shop they loved. They often come out to say hello in their own way to friends, customers, and to Debi herself.

To be fair, I should begin by telling you that there have been no less than four deaths in the house attached to the Rock Shop. The tenants before Bill and Gean had a mother in law who was ill and who passed away there. Then Bill and Gean's own mother died in the home. Bill departed this world in May and Gean didn't have the will to live without him. She managed to hang on through her son's birthday, then went into a coma the next day and died exactly three weeks after her beloved Bill. So in all, there were indeed four deaths that we know of in the house, and all died peacefully of natural causes. Oh... and there was a dog that passed away as well. More on that in a moment.

Soon after her adoptive parents left the physical world, Debi began to experience strange phenomena. She spotted Bill walking up and down the sidewalk outside several times and still does to this day. When she goes to investigate, however, he is never there. He also likes to show up from time to time in pictures taken in the house. And his presence can be felt often.

Gean is just as lively and fun in death as she was in life. She plays tricks on Debi and on the customers that come in. One of her favorite things to do is to tug on Debi's right earring and on more than one occasion she has pulled it completely out of Debi's ear and sent it flying across the room in full view of a customer. Gean also hides the store keys from time to time unless Debi asks her not to. Gean has also been known to move Debi's decorative rocks around in her home. It seems she also has a fondness for one of Debi's favorite crystals that is kept in a box in the home. Sometimes when Debi goes to look for it, it is sometimes there in the box, but sometimes not. She says if it is not there when she looks, she just puts the box back in its place and waits a few days. When she goes back to check on it, the crystal is back as if it had never been gone.

But Gean does more than play tricks and games to let herself be known. She also appeared in a mirror when a picture was taken during a ghost hunt in the house. And her voice was captured talking quite a bit to the ghost hunters about their investigation. Her son, Robert, found a birthday card, made out to him, and signed by Gean exactly one year after her death in a place it could not have hidden all year. She has also been seen standing and moving about in one corner of the shop, and Debi has felt her disapproval when some paperwork did not get done as it should. But Debi says Gean also comforts her from time to time in such ways as patting her on the back when she has had some trouble or gotten into an argument. She also gives off a calming feeling when Debi is stressed.

During the ghost hunt, the investigators captured many pictures with vibrant orbs in them. Debi says that is very common in the house and shop. They also captured a picture of a man with a beard. No one knows who the man was, but he seems to have wandered into the mix somehow. And then of course, there is the dog.

At one time the Wheless family owned a little white dog named "Dixie." It was a beloved pet and there was a lot of sadness when Dixie passed away. But like other living things that meet their demise in the home, Dixie managed to hang around without the need for a corporeal body. The dog has been seen running through the house and has come up to people to be petted – but when they reach down to do so, Dixie is not there. Debi said she has seen, heard, and felt the dog so many times she reaches to pet it absentmindedly now and is disappointed when her hand meets empty air. She related to me that Dixie will get in bed with her quite often, and once or twice she actually witnessed the impressions appearing on the bed covers as the spirit-dog walked across them. She went on to say that her living dog plays with Dixie all the time. The whole experience has gone from the amazing to the accepted as part of the program that comes with living in the house attached to the shop.

Not everything is peachy keen all the time, however. Once a spirit got in the abode that was clearly not a nice guy. Debi was bending over to pick up her basket of laundry, when a picture that had hung on the wall for years suddenly fell/flew forward, hitting her on the head and shoulder before sliding over her and landing on her feet, breaking two of her toes. By that point she had seen so many unexplainable things happen in the house, that rather than get freaked out, she got mad. She picked up the picture and broke it in to pieces and said out loud that that was unacceptable behavior and she was not going to put up with it. Being already in motion, she picked up the basket and headed to the laundry room, griping all the way.

When she reached the washer, she began putting her clothes inside and once again loudly reprimanded whatever spirit had hit her with picture. There were two green tables in the laundry room with a few things sitting on them and as soon as Debi verbalized her anger, one of the tables slid across the room and hit her leg. This angered her more and without thinking she said: "That's pretty good... now why don't you hit me with the other one!" And as if it were a genie answering a wish, the second table slid into her. The anger left her and fear replaced it. She decided it was time to get out of the house for a while.

She went looking for her friend, Mary Lowery. Mary is a Shaman and is 91 years old. She is experienced in many things paranormal, including identifying and removing unwanted spirits. Unfortunately, Mary was not at home, so Debi returned to the house and her unfinished laundry.

When she entered the room she tried not to think about what had happened and went about her chores. The spirit wasn't through with her, unfortunately, and quickly let her know it was still there. An empty box of Petron flew off the high shelf it had set on for years and came across the room to hit Debi in the head. That was too much to deal with. She yelled her disapproval and left the house again in search of her friend, determined not to return without her.

Luckily, this time, Mary was found and returned to the house with Debi. Mary quickly identified the troublesome spirit as an outsider who had just wandered in. And she was able to banish him from the home. Debi hasn't had any trouble from unwanted spiritual guests since, but she says if she ever does, she knows who to call.

In my many visits to the place, I have never experienced anything physical or visual that I would call paranormal. But I have been awed by the strong sense of peace in the place. I have had the sense that there were more people in the room than I could see. And I have felt welcome from the moment my foot hit the doorway. And yes, I get a hug from Debi when I come in, just as all Gean's customers got from her. Everyone is welcomed to the family at the Crystal Rock Shop.

The Crystal Rock Shop is located at 2136 Roy Road in Tyler, Texas 75707. The hours of operation are 10AM to 6PM on Friday and Saturday only. You may give Debi a call during her business hours at 903-581-7750. And be sure to check out the shop's Facebook page by looking up crystalrockshoptyler2.

Bigfoot in Tyler

Ah, the legendary bigfoot… these big, hairy beasts have been spotted from the Himalayas to the Hawaiian Islands, from the Pacific Northwest to the panhandle of Florida. The creatures have been the subject of horror movies, comedic feature films, and even used to sell beef jerky on television. No matter what you think about bigfoot, he (or she, whichever) has become a part of popular culture today.

So what place does the secretive sasquatch have in a ghost book? Amazingly enough, the topic has found itself well under the umbrella of the paranormal. Attend any paranormal conference, and a cryptozoologist is always an interesting part of the program – probably because the people who are so open to the existence of a spirit world beyond our own are also not only willing to entertain the idea of unknown creatures in our physical world, are also extremely curious about the subject.

And with that in mind, it must be mentioned that bigfoot is no stranger to the Tyler area. That fact probably shouldn't surprise anyone; after all, there are some twelve million acres of forest in the Lone Star State, most of it in the pineywoods of East Texas. The region boasts four national forests and five state forests all maintained in their natural state – the perfect home for creatures wishing to avoid contact with the world... and the city of Tyler and Smith County lies nestled there among the pine trees.

Instead of relying on lore and legend, some of the leading cryptozoological organizations were consulted to see just what kind of bigfoot activity has been reported around Tyler... and as it turns out, the stories go back at least fifty years. Here are some of the reports in the area...

Fall, 1963 – Several young men were out in the Marlow Bottoms just south of Tyler coon-hunting. It was a cold, dark evening, just about midnight. The dogs began to bark as if they'd treed a raccoon, but when the men approached to examine their prey, they saw a large, bipedal animal standing before them covered in reddish fur, and surrounded by the dogs. It was waving its arms and howling in either rage or fear. One of the men shot at it, bringing another loud howl, and the young men fled, followed by the dogs. (as documented by the Bigfoot Field Researchers Organization, www.bfro.net)

June, 1972 – A grandfather and his grandsons were on their way home from fishing at Lake Tyler. The sun was just starting to go down. As they came to a clearing where they had stopped to pick wild plums in the past, there appeared to be a gray horse rearing up on its hind legs. As they got closer, it became clear that the animal was not a horse, but instead a humanoid creature standing about seven feet tall. It turned and walked away, arms swinging as it moved, with its knees slightly bent. There was no hair on the face, and its skin there and on its palms was dark brown. As the creature came to the tree line, it stepped over a five-strand barbed wire fence in stride. The grandfather turned the car around, and warned the boys not to tell anyone about the incident. (as documented by the Gulf Coast Bigfoot Research Organization, www.gcbro.com)

Spring, 1973 – An engaged couple were parked at Lake Palestine late one evening, when they heard rustling noises in the brush around the car. It alarmed them, so the man started the car and put it into reverse to leave. As they looked back, the back-up lights illuminated a large creature that was standing on two feet. Because their car was a Volkswagen low to the ground, they only saw it from the waist down before it fled with more rustling of leaves and branches. (as documented by the North American Wood Ape Conservancy, woodape.org)

May 1998 – A young lady was at her rural home outside Tyler one evening playing video games. It was late, and her parents had already gone to bed. She suddenly heard a loud breathing coming from outside the window, which she first attributed to her dogs. When it stopped, she decided to check on the dogs to make sure that they were all right. Instead of being outside of the window, she finally located them huddled in the garage, apparently afraid to come out - since they were watch dogs, it was a situation extremely out of character for them. When she went back inside the house, she began to hear loud banging noises from outside, so she woke her parents. After her father got his gun, the three of them stepped outside to find massive limbs in the front yard. The limbs were clearly too heavy for a person to lift. Although no one was around, there was a terrible smell in the air. (as documented by the Gulf Coast Bigfoot Research Organization, www.gcbro.com)

June, 2001 – On the east side of Lake Tyler, three boys were fishing at a local creek, and decided to call it a day when it began to get dark. As they walked away, one of them realized that he'd left their bait behind; he ran back to get it, but then returned in a panic reporting a man-like beast covered with light-colored hair. When the trio went back, they saw the

69

creature, which immediately jumped the creek and fled into the woods. According to one of the witnesses, the creek was too wide to be jumped by a man. A short time later, kids involved in a paintball game in the same area spotted the same creature. It hadn't noticed them, so they quickly fled. (as documented by the Bigfoot Field Researchers Organization, www.bfro.net)

February, 2002 – At approximately 3 AM at a rural home in Smith County, the family dogs began to bark in alarm. The owner of the house went outside with his rifle and large flashlight. He heard the horses in the pasture were panicking, so he swept the field with the light. The dog ran out to investigate, but then abruptly turned and ran back to the house. The night was then filled with the sounds of limbs crashing and brush rustling as a seemingly large animal left the area. A month or so later, the event repeated with the dog alerting the family and the owner once again coming outside with his gun and light. As he searched the field, he saw trees waving as if something huge had just walked through them. He went to the scene and found the grass crushed down as if the beast had been stepping over the fence there. There was also a strong scent in the air that the man described as a mixture of skunk and rotting meat. As he returned to the house, there was a low scream that seemed to be about a hundred yards into the woods. Although the man was familiar with the howls of all of the indigenous animals, the one that he heard was completely unfamiliar. (as documented by the North American Wood Ape Conservancy, www.woodape.org)

January, 2004 – A young man was riding a four-wheeler on a wooded ranch near Tyler. He was following a trail beside a fence-line, going approximately 20 MPH, when he heard pounding footsteps keeping pace beside him. He saw trees and brush moving, but never saw what was shadowing him. He came back to the location on the same four-wheeler a week or so later, this time at night. As he rounded a corner on the trail, the headlights lit up a dark figure with two shining eyes standing about seven feet tall – it suddenly disappeared into the night. More time passed, and the young man was back riding the trail after a rain, when the four-wheeler became stuck in the mud. As he was working to pull it out, there was a long, mournful cry from the woods – something that he'd never heard before. (as documented by the Bigfoot Field Researchers Organization, www.bfro.net)

March, 2011 – Around 2 AM, in a rural, wooded area near Tyler, a witness heard the call of an animal that made the hair on the back of his neck stand up. Shortly thereafter, he heard a higher-pitched call as if in reply, but from a distance away. Family members heard the same strange cry in the night. (as documented by the Bigfoot Field Researchers Organization, www.bfro.net)

April, 2011 – A man was driving along County Road 129 just outside of Tyler, when a creature ran across the road in front of his car. It appeared to be at least six feet tall, with a dark orange hair covering its body. The witness reported that the sighting was "disturbing." Not long after that, the same witness along with his son saw the same type of beast standing at the edge of a wooded area. It stood there for 10-15 seconds, before turning and disappearing into the woods. (as documented by the Bigfoot Field Researchers Organization, www.bfro.net)

These sightings are some that have been reported around Tyler and Smith County – there are certainly many that are discounted by witnesses, or that go unreported because the person who had the experience it is afraid of ridicule.

The accounts reported here share similar points – the hair on the beast is gray or red, there is a pungent odor associated with the experience, the creature is large enough to easily move aside trees and brush, and even easily step over a fence. The howl produced is low and unlike anything the witnesses had heard before. Fortunately, none of the people were harmed in the course of their encounters.

They were frightened, however... but who wouldn't be, when facing the legendary creature that we call bigfoot.

The Cherokee Trace Pt. 1:
Haunting & Creatures

As a teenager, I learned to drive on some of the most interesting little oil top roads in East Texas. Before I even had a license, I would sneak out in my daddy's car in the middle of the night and carefully ease along these backroads for about six miles... the distance between my house and my girlfriend's. The roads were narrow, and dark as a cave at night. Passing another car was sometimes an interesting chore on these trails, but they always got me where I wanted to go without ever having to get out on a main road.

Growing up, I learned that quite a few of these roads were known as the Cherokee Trace. The Cherokee Trace was a historic trail that traversed East and Northeast Texas. The Native American tribe known as the Cherokee is credited with blazing this route in about 1821. This can't really be proven for sure however, as stories persist that the trace may have evolved from trails marked by other Native American groups, or French traders a century earlier, and that the Cherokees only further defined and smoothed out this course. According to folklore, the Indians dragged buffalo skins behind their horses to flatten the tall grass, clearing the path of brush and logs as they went. They made sure the road went by the best camping places, river fords, and springs. They also planted honeysuckle and rose bushes along the route. The white blooming rows of flowers functioned as bright and effective indicators of the trace. Due to the stiff hardiness of the plant, the "Cherokee Rose" later became recognized and utilized by settlers as a dependable shrub for fencing.

The trail ran from what is now Nacogdoches up through Tyler and Northeast Texas including Gregg, Upshur, and Camp counties. The road then crossed Big Cypress Creek into Titus County near the historic location of Fort Sherman and continued north to Indian settlements in Oklahoma and Arkansas. Having a dual function as both a travel and trading route for East Texas Indians, the trail also enabled the migration of many settlers into Texas. Legend has it that Sam Houston, David Crockett, and other participants in the Texas Revolution first crossed the Red River into Texas on the Cherokee Trace. Early land grant surveys of the 1830s and 1840s mention the trail and define roads that evolved from this route such as the Fort Towson Road and Clarksville-Nacogdoches Road.

There are many stories of hauntings and mysterious happenings occurring on the Trace. There are tales of Native American spirits, giant birds, the "lady of the road," bigfoot, strange creatures, aliens, haunted houses, and of course there is the story of "the Pig Man." Some stem from Indian legends, others are rooted in more recent personal experiences by travelers. Some sound so farfetched as to be fairy tales, but a couple of the incidents related in these stories I have experienced myself while driving these lonely backroads.

First there are the stories of the spirits. The reports are too numerous to count of folks seeing Cherokee Indians walking along the road, sometimes vanishing in plain sight. The most interesting story is that of a young man walking home by way of the trace during the 1930s. He had gotten about two miles into a four-mile walk when he heard the sound of drums coming from up ahead around the bend. It was late in the day, but the sun had not fully set yet. He walked around the curve and saw four Native Americans in full war garb dancing around a fifth who was pounding on a drum. He said they held spears and looked very angry. When they noticed him, they stopped their dance, stood motionless, and stared at the young white man who had entered their camp. One of the Indians screamed what was later described by the young man as a "nightmare call from hell" and charged at him brandishing his spear, eyes brimming with hatred. It happened so fast there was nothing for him to do but close his eyes and brace for the impact of the spear piercing his body. So close his eyes he did, and tried to hurriedly make his peace with God – but nothing happened. When he opened his eyes again, the Indians were gone, as if they had never been there. There were no tracks to be found. There was not one sign that there had been a war dance going on or any other kind of gathering. They had just vanished. The young fellow burst into a run and did not stop until he reached his home. Since then, the sound of war drums coming from near the road has been heard many times. And Indian warriors have supposedly charged out of the bushes threatening an attack on both pedestrians and vehicles alike, only to disappear before damage can be done.

There is a story that goes around from time to time about a giant bird that nests along the Trace. As the reports go it is black with red eyes and three times as big as the biggest vulture you have ever seen. It has been sighted numerous times flying low to the ground, skimming over the tops of cars, and making a screeching noise that will turn your blood cold. One person even swore it had tried to attack his car and then flew away.

Yet another interesting fact related to me about the Trace is that a number of people have sworn to have spotted bigfoot along the path and in the nearby woods – mirroring some of the same stories that I shared in a previous chapter on the legendary beast. Folks say that such a big, hairy creature wanders through the area of the Trace and is sometimes heard crashing through the undergrowth and growling before it is ever seen. Most times the noises stop before there is a sighting, as if the creature becomes aware it is not alone and freezes in place. Unexplained howling noises in the night have also been attributed to this creature through the years.

In one of the areas along the trail where there is a fairly high bridge, it is said you can come face to face with "the lady of the road." The story goes that she was in her twenties sometime near the turn of the century, and had been murdered and her body dumped off the bridge by her lover. It seems she knew quite a bit about a crime he had committed and had begged him to turn himself in. When he refused, she told him she loved him too much to see him throw away his life with a criminal career, so she decided to go and report him herself. She reasoned that he might do a little time, learn an important lesson, and she would be waiting for him to begin a new life when he was released. Apparently she didn't know him as well as she thought she did, or maybe his love for himself was deeper than his love for her, because he strangled her on the spot. Two days after he had weighed down her body and dumped it into the water below the bridge, a fisherman somehow hooked into her garments and dragged enough of her to the surface to see what he had snagged. The investigation was short, as everyone knew where she had been when she disappeared. Her man was brought to justice. From that point on, the poor misguided soul of the strangled lady can be seen walking along the road near the bridge. Sometimes people drive on past without a thought, but on the occasions when people stop to offer her a ride, they always get the same story. She is trying to get back to her man to stop him from doing something terrible. She is always distraught and after telling people of her mission, she usually vanishes.

My father had very few stories to tell me growing up. He was a farmer and rancher and kept life pretty well balanced between work and sleep. There wasn't much time for anything else. But one of the stories I did coax from him during a rare moment at the dinner table was of the abandoned house that use to sit on the Trace near the Sabine River Bottoms.

My father built many of the roads in East Texas in his youth before he settled into farming. His first real job was operating a drag line. He would often leave his parents sleeping and head out for work long before daylight. He could sometimes catch a ride to work, but more often than not he was the last man to leave whatever road construction site they were on for the day and ended up walking home. Being very familiar with East Texas roads, he was a master at finding the shortest route to get from point A to point B. Sometimes this involved traveling down oil or dirt roads, and on occasion he even cut across fields and through wooded areas.

It was an evening such as this that found him walking along the Cherokee Trace as he headed home. He had walked this route several times before and knew it well. He and his brothers often hunted in the woods around the Trace and he felt very at home there. The fact that he was one quarter Cherokee Indian probably didn't hurt either. He had gotten to the part of the Trace between Gilmer and Bettie, Texas he referred to as "the cave roads" because the trees grew tall on either side and the limbs stretched across and met over the road to give the effect of being in a leafy cavern. It was dark out as the sun had set about thirty minutes earlier. He only had about thirty more minutes of walking before he reached home and he was tired so he didn't move very fast, but rather maintained a decent stride as he put more and more of the Trace behind him.

This was during the late 1940s and there were not very many houses along the trail, and fewer lights of any kind. There was an abandoned farm house sitting off the road about forty feet or so that he had passed by before wondering why no one had moved in and fixed it up. It was nothing fancy, one story, wood frame, with a decent yard and picket fence around it. It looked like the kind of place a hard-working, small family could enjoy and call home. However, it had been abandoned for a long time and it was beginning to show signs of disrepair. The paint was peeling off everywhere, some of the fence had collapsed, a window had been broken out, and the roof looked like it might have a leak or two.

As he neared the house this time, the moon began to shine down on him and he could see clearly despite the tree canopy over his head. He began to hear music coming from the abandoned house and saw that there were lights on inside it. He could even see the silhouettes of people moving across the curtains as if they were dancing. He guessed someone had taken advantage of the fact that the home was empty and had decided to throw a party there. Or, he reasoned, it was finally being lived in, and this was a house warming gathering. If it was locals throwing a party, he figured he had about a ninety percent chance of knowing someone there since he knew just about everybody in the surrounding area. If it was a housewarming he figured he would like to say hello and introduce himself as he was pretty sure he would pass this way many times in the future and they might be kind enough to offer him a drink, a rest, or a ride on his journey home. Either way, he decided he would stop and ask for a glass of water and see what was going on.

As he approached the house, the music became louder and he could hear that it was big band swing music and was very lively. He could see the shadows on the curtains more clearly and could tell they were indeed dancing. He opened the gate and walked up the path to the three steps that led up to the porch. He could hear laughter and people's voices now. He stepped onto the porch and made his way to the screen door. He opened it and knocked on the wooden door behind it.

As soon as his knuckles made the first knock, the lights went out instantly. The music stopped. The voices were silent. There was not a sound to be heard except the wind blowing through the nearby trees. At first he was stunned. He listened closely but could hear no movement inside the home either. He knocked again and again but no one came to the door and when he tested the knob he found it was locked. So, he gave up. He decided it must be a private party and he wasn't wanted, and he began to leave.

He left the porch and traversed the path to the gate in the picket fence. He opened the gate and went out, allowing it close behind him. As soon as the gate closed, the lights in the house came back on, the music roared to life and again he could hear people talking and laughing. He thought maybe he had just frightened them. Maybe they thought he was a lawman and they didn't want their party busted. Or maybe they thought he was a transient and didn't want to deal with him. With these thoughts in mind, he decided to give it another shot.

He entered the gated yard again, and walked toward the porch. This time, he called out that he was not a cop and was not a transient. As he climbed the steps he proclaimed aloud that he was their neighbor and was just stopping to introduce himself and maybe get a glass of water. After stepping onto the porch, he went to the screen door, opened it, and knocked again, calling out greetings in a friendly voice. Unfortunately, as before, the lights and music instantly went off. The voices and laughter died, and was replaced with utter silence. He called out that he meant no harm. He told whoever might be listening that he was a friend. It was all of little use, as all that greeted his ears was more silence.

79

Angry now, and thinking that either someone was playing a mean spirited trick on him, or that the folks inside were just jerks, he came up with a plan. Having tried the knob again and testing the strength of the door, he saw that it had fallen in to such a sad state that it wouldn't take much to knock it down. He told himself that if the music and lights came on again before he got out of sight of the house, he was going to charge up there and break the door down and find out who was hiding from him and why they didn't want him to join their party.

Grumbling his discontent, he left the porch, went down the little path, and opened the fence gate to let himself out. Again, as soon as the gate closed behind him, the house roared to life. Now, my dad was very muscular and agile when he was young, and mom used to say he kept wound so tight that he could spring with the speed of a wild cat at any moment he chose. That is exactly what he did at that moment. Without any hesitation, and before the little gate could even bounce back fully into place, he jumped over it, hurtled up the path like a rocket, cleared the steps up to the porch in one leap and crashed through the screen door and the wooden door at the same time, knocking them both inward in a shower of splinters.

I will never forget the look on his face as he got to this point in his story. His eyes got big, and he looked at me without a hint of emotion on his face. His voice lowered and I felt like he was really trying to impress upon me how serious and truthful he was being with me then. It frightened me a bit because I knew he was not making this up.

He told me that the instant that door gave way, the lights and music died again, and the voices stopped. He said it became dark and quiet as a tomb and he lay on top of the broken doors in the front room of the house and looked around wildly for someone to hit. You see, the lights hadn't quite gone out fast enough. He had caught just the most fleeting of glimpses into the room before it went dark. He saw the people in there...and they didn't look right. He said they had blood on them and they looked like "dead things." Though after he was in the house, he couldn't see anything in the room with him, and the moonlight was bright enough that he certainly would have if there had been someone to see, he felt their presence. And he felt like something in this empty room was about to get him.

He launched himself into a screaming roll out the shattered doorway and came to his feet in time to nearly fly off the porch. He said he couldn't even remember opening the fence gate when he got to it. He said he must have either leapt over it or crashed right through it. All he could think about at the time was getting the hell away from that house and whatever party guests were inside it. He didn't stay in the vicinity long enough to note whether the music came back on again or not. He ran like a runaway train the rest of the way home.

My father never went by that house again. He refused to travel down that part of the Trace again until years later when he found out the house had been torn down and nature had pretty much reclaimed the home site. I never doubted his story. My father didn't speak much in general, and no one ever knew the man to fabricate anything.

I have since been able to come reasonably close to pinpointing where this house used to sit. There is an old well off the road, in the woods, and a few bricks laying here and there that probably made up the foundation. I got a few chills while I was there. And I wondered what exactly my father had seen there that night so many years ago. Since he has passed away, I will never get the chance to ask him anything else about it. It looks like this is one party I missed, and probably for the best.

Artist's rendition of the Pig Man of the Trace

The Cherokee Trace Pt. 2:
Legend of the Pig Man

There is an old story that has been passed down through the years about a mentally-challenged man who met a terrible fate on the Cherokee Trace. I first heard it when I was a teenager out on a double date with my girlfriend, my best friend, and his girl. The four of us were driving around the back roads of East Texas, looking for a good place to park and make out when someone suggested telling ghost stories to get us in the mood to snuggle and hold each other tight. My friend piped up that he had a story for us that was not made up, but would make the hair on the back of our necks stand up. He related the story I present to you now.

Somewhere around 1900, a black man was born in his family home on the Cherokee Trace not far outside of Tyler,

Texas. No one seems to know exactly where this home was, as it was torn down when the last family member passed away in the 1950s. This young man had it rough from the beginning. His mother died in childbirth and he was born with a mental defect due to almost suffocating in the womb. Physically, he was healthy and well, but his mind never operated beyond a first grade level. His father dubbed him "Junior" when he was born and that was all anyone ever called him, but his given first name was "Buford."

He worked hard for and with his father from the time he was old enough to stand on his own. They were incredibly poor, and a black man in the South in those days, never had it easy. Every day was a day of labor from dawn to dusk just to make sure they were able to eat and make ends meet. This often meant doing any kind of job they could get for very little pay. Yet, even though their tiny house looked as if a strong wind might blow it over and times were harsh, they managed to survive.

The father was sometimes harsh and rough on the boy. He resented the fact that his wife had passed away delivering a son that would never be a man. Junior grew fast and usually wore clothing that had been patched over and over, often given to him from someone who had already worn it out. He was seen in overalls that were too short for his long legs, with no shirt, trundling along behind his father. And though the boy did manage to keep up with his father and grew to be big and tall and strong as an ox, he never really won his father's love. It was a sad existence and perhaps it was this lack of affection that drove the young man to seek out any sort of recognition he could find.

When he turned twenty-two, prohibition was in full swing, and folks along the Trace began making a little extra money by distilling moonshine. One such person was a local pig farmer by the name of Randall. He had often used Junior to help feed slop to the pigs and to clean the pens – basically to do all the disgusting jobs that Randall didn't want to do himself. So when Randall began making shine, he naturally recruited Junior to help him deliver it, figuring if they were caught, it would be Junior that took the fall.

Junior didn't seem to mind. I am not even sure if he knew that what he was doing was illegal. As big and tough as he looked, he was still just a child inside, and he told Randall he would do anything he wanted him to do as long as Randall kept allowing him to help take care of the pigs. Junior had come to think of the pigs as pets. He even had names for each one of them, and would talk to them while he fed them or worked around their pens. Often he was seen sitting in the pen petting the pigs and playing with them as if they were puppies. Of course, he would get filthy doing this, and folks began to call him "Pig Man" as a derogatory title. Junior didn't care about that either. He loved his pigs and wore the name with pride. He took to calling himself "Pig Man Junior" and came up with a little song about it he would sing to himself while he worked or walked to and from the pig pens.

People as a rule, can be very mean when they have a mind to be, and children, especially teenagers, can be the meanest of them all. You see, Randall had a teenage son that despised Junior. He didn't like the fact that this "boy in the body of a man" could out-work him, and was slowly becoming a better companion to his father than his own son – even if that companionship was really just an excuse to get Junior to run shine. The teenager taunted Junior relentlessly and became furious when nothing he said seemed to have any effect on the black man. Soon he was getting his teenage friends to come over and help taunt Junior. They played cruel tricks on him when they could. But no matter what, as long as Junior got to spend time with his pigs, he never showed any sign of being bothered.

Finally the teenager could take no more. He stole the latest batch of moonshine from his father and told the lie that Junior had taken it. He got his teenage friends to lie as well and tell Randall they had seen Junior leave with it. They went so far as to say they had seen him sell it and take the money to his own father.

Things were different back in those days... things happened that should not have, and people got away with things that would put them in jail today. Randall believed his son. And when Junior showed up that day to take care of the pigs, Randall, his son, and the other teenagers beat him mercilessly and made him crawl off the property.

Junior did not understand this. He knew he didn't take the moonshine, but in his childlike mind, he reasoned he must have done something bad to make them mad at him. He decided he would try to make it up to them any way he could. He just couldn't stand to be away from his beloved pigs. Believing that a gift of some sort would make things better, he took what little food he and his father had left in the house and mashed it up into a slop bucket to take to the pig farm. He was going to tell Mr. Randall that it was the finest slop in town and it would make his pigs grow big and pretty. He figured this was a sure way to get back in Randall's good graces... even if it meant going hungry himself.

As soon as he was satisfied with the bucket of slop, and even though he was sore and bruised all over from the beating he had taken the day before, he set out on foot to walk the two miles to the pig farm, carrying the bucket with him. He sang his little "Pig Man Junior" song as loud as he could to keep his spirits up as he walked.

Unfortunately, Randall's son and a couple of his buddies were driving down the Trace at that moment in their old Model A truck. When they saw Junior walking and heard him singing they slowed to a crawl beside him and began to yell at him and tell him to shut up and go back home. He kept singing even when they yelled at him that his name was not "Pig Man," or even "Junior," but rather "Buford" and nobody cared.

Eventually, when the singing didn't stop, one of the boys jumped out of the slow moving truck and came over and knocked Junior to the ground, spilling his "fine slop" all over the ground.

Junior began to cry and scoop the slop off the ground with his hands and try to put it back in the bucket. He had stopped singing and he clearly heard the boys laughing at him as they started to drive away. Something inside him snapped and he threw a handful of slop at them as they drove off. I guess some of the slop hit them or hit the truck, because they noticed it immediately and slammed on the brakes. Seeing this, Junior knew he was in trouble, and grabbing up his bucket, he began to run for home.

The boys in the truck decided to teach Junior a lesson once and for all. They spun the truck around and gassed it, heading for him. At this point in the story, it becomes muddled whether they had a baseball bat, a two by four, or an ax. Whatever the case, their plan was to drive by him at top speed and pummel him with their weapon. This plan was put into action as fast as they could get the truck pointed in Junior's direction.

I can't say how fast they were going. I have no idea exactly what weapon they used. But according to the story I have heard many times since that first evening, they were going very fast, and Randall's son leaned out the truck door, calling out to Junior just as the vehicle drew even with him. Sadly, Junior stopped and turned to see what they wanted, as a child might do. The weapon was traveling at the truck's speed, plus the speed of the swing by the punk teen, and when it connected with Junior it hit his neck. It was so hard a blow that it either sheared his head completely, off or took a large part of his head off, depending on which version of the story you hear. Junior fell dead in the ditch beside the Cherokee Trace... and the murderers drove on without looking back.

Someone saw the body and went and got Junior's father. When they came back upon the scene, Junior's head was missing. Some folks said an animal had smelled the blood and had come and drug it off. Others said the teenagers had come back and picked it up and had taken it and fed it to the pigs that Junior had loved so much. Either way, it was never found and Buford Junior, the Pig Man was laid to rest without it.

About a month after this horrible crime, justice had not been served. Even though everyone strongly suspected who had committed the act, there were no outside witnesses. The boys manufactured an alibi, even getting Randall to vouch for the truth of it. As I said before, things were different then and sometimes things happened that were not right. In this case, it looked like the miscreants were going to get away with murder.

Another month passed and one night Randall's son did not come home. The next morning he was found in a ditch on the side of the Trace. His head was missing... and there was a slop bucket under the torso, catching the blood as it left through the gaping wound that had been a neck. That is when the legend really began.

Folks began to whisper that Junior had come back to get his revenge. They said he sought and found a way to have his own justice. And they said he found himself a new head at the same time. Other folks believed that Junior's father had exacted justice himself... that maybe he did love his mentally challenged son after all, enough to kill the killer. There were, again, no witnesses and no evidence to go on. And frankly there was just enough of a supernatural element to it that folks decided not to dig too deep. It was best to let sleeping pigs lie.

After the second murder, people in the area began seeing Junior again. Frightened witnesses said they saw Junior's body walking along the road at night carrying his slop bucket, but they said the body had no head. People said they could hear someone singing the "Pig Man Junior" song on the road at night. And folks began to fear to be out too late. Folks even began to be afraid to do business with Randall at the pig farm because they didn't want to do anything that would bring down the wrath of the headless Pig Man on them. This eventually caused Randall to go bankrupt and sell off all his pigs at market. In order to try to make back the huge amounts of money he lost on his pigs, he increased his moonshine productions tenfold. This caught the attention of the authorities, and Randall was soon arrested and sent to jail for bootlegging. Justice was finally completely served.

To this day, people swear they see the headless body of a black man in too-small overalls walking along the road at night. They say he carries a bucket. And often they hear a funny little song coming from somewhere... some say it seems to come from the bucket the man carries...as if he carries his own missing head in it. Modern teens terrorize each other with this story and say it's not good to be out at night because the Pig Man might take a liking to your head and decide he wants it for his own. And often they dare each other to stop beside the road in the dark and call "Here, piggy piggy!" I don't know what response they get or expect to get from this, but I know you won't catch me out there calling pigs in the dark. Whether Junior still wanders the night looking for his head and his pigs or not, my friend was right about one thing – when he was done telling us this story, every hair on my neck was standing at attention.

Artist's rendition of the Flying Ship of the Trace

The Cherokee Trace Pt. 3:
The Strange Flying Ship

I suppose it is fitting that I had my own weird experience on the Cherokee Trace, much as my father had years before. As I have mentioned earlier, I learned to drive on these roads and used to sneak over to my girlfriend's house late at night when I could. I was coming home from one such adventure when something happened that I have never shared before. However, since I am writing about the Trace, and since I have received encouragement from my dear friend, Texas UFO Researcher Sunny Williams, I have decided to share my story.

It was a summer night in 1988 and I was in my father's 1986 Buick, blaring the radio and singing at the top of my lungs to *Rock Me Amadeus* by Falco as I drove down the lonely

91

parts of the Cherokee Trace. I was happy and life seemed pretty darn good. I was thinking about my date that night and about work the next morning, and little else as I motored along. I had passed the last of the homes along the road for several miles and was entering a low place near the river bottoms. There was a particular part of the road here where it went downhill suddenly and then crossed three small bridges over creek beds that were very close together. I enjoyed this part of the ride because if you hit it at a decent speed, the sudden drop and then rise and drop succession felt like a roller coaster. So, as I saw it coming, I sped up.

The car felt like it dropped out from under me as I hit the sudden downhill slope and my stomach lurched as a thrill ran through me. I hit the first bridge quickly after and experienced the same sensation as I went up and over. The second bridge gave me the same effect but when I crossed it, my car started to die. It rumbled, shuddered, jerked, and fell silent as I coasted to the edge of the road just before the third bridge. As it rolled to a stop, the radio and lights died too, including the entire dashboard.

I set there for a minute trying to figure out what to do. It was almost one in the morning and I was no mechanic. It was pitch black down in the middle of the river bottoms, and I had no flashlight. The nearest house was nearly a mile away and I did not relish the thought of walking up to it in the middle of the night to try to get help. All these thoughts went flying out of my head as I looked up and saw something odd over the tops of the trees across the road in front of me.

Hovering what seemed like only a few feet above the trees was some kind of ship. No, it was not a saucer-shaped craft as so many people have seen before. It looked like a large triangle with the nose point cut off. It had lights on each corner and a long strip of light going down the middle of the underneath. It seemed to be emitting some kind of heat, because it looked like there was a heat haze near the rear underside. It just hung there, floating, not making any sound at all. If I had to guess how big it was, I would say it was about the length of a commercial airplane, but it was as wide as a four lane highway. It was big, and I could see that it was made of some kind of dull metal.

I tried in desperation to start the engine on the car but it wouldn't even make an attempt to turn over. I was stuck. And oddly enough, even though I was in a freaky predicament, I don't remember being scared... just anxious. I probably should have been shaking like a leaf, but somehow I kept calm and watched the hovering ship. The strip of light under the center of it began to get brighter. It seemed to get incredibly, unreasonably bright. The area I was in was lit up brighter than daylight. For some reason that I don't understand, I chose this moment to open the car door and step out.

I have no idea what happened next. It's not like I blacked out, or was so scared I mentally blocked it out. It is as if the memory is just not there. The next thing I remember is realizing I was back in my car and the engine was running and I was driving along the Trace. When I snapped awake, for lack of a better term, I was about a mile further down the road and was passing the first few houses of the next stretch of inhabited area.

I tried to remember what had just happened, but it would not come to me. I clearly remember everything up to the bright light and getting out of the car... and that's it. At that point I did what I'm sure no other person on the planet would have done. I slammed on my breaks, whipped the car around in somebody's yard, and gassed the engine as I sped back to the scene of my experience. I was determined to find out what happened and I wanted to see if the ship was still there. I guess most folks would have been grateful to be back in their vehicles heading home. But I've always been the type that if something messes with me too much, I mess back. Because of that, and my undying sense of curiosity, I knew I would never forgive myself if I did not immediately return to the spot.

It only took a moment to reach the bridges again in the low river bottoms. I slowed and pulled over to the side of the road where I remembered the car dying before. There was no ship over the trees. There were no lights. Everything was calm and still. I began to doubt myself. I wondered if I had imagined the whole thing... if perhaps I'd had a seizure, or dozed off for just a second while driving. Two things happened at that point to convince me something had taken place there that was not only weird, but probably not of this world.

First, I happened to look down at the clock on the dashboard. There were two of them there. One was digital and was wired into the electric system of the car. It said it was just a little after 1AM, the time it should be. The second clock was a small independent unit that my dad had stuck to the dash for whatever reason. This second clock said it was about 2:30AM. There was about an hour and a half difference between the two and I had no idea which was right. They had both been set the same earlier. I had made sure of it, to be on time for my date and the movie we went to see. Later, when I got home, I found out the second clock was right. I had lost over an hour of time to... what?

Secondly, as I pondered the clock differential, I noticed something lying on the ground in front of my car. I got out, leaving the car running and the headlights on, and went to see what it was. What I found laying on the ground was my own wallet. I realized it had not been my imagination. I had been there a short time before and my wallet had somehow fallen out. But I still could not remember the missing segment of time. After looking around briefly, and deciding I wasn't quite as brave as I had felt a minute ago, I got back in the Buick, turned it around, and headed home at a decent clip.

I didn't tell my folks about it. I hinted at it days later and they started acting a little strange when I did, so I let it go. I tried to tell my best friend about it, but he made a joke about me probably being "probed." It embarrassed and angered me so that I decided not to talk about it ever again – until now. After hearing so many other stories similar to mine that happened to people right here in East Texas, as we looked at in a previous chapter, and after meeting and befriending Sunny Williams the UFO researcher, I felt better about sharing my experience.

Several times after this happened to me, and still to this day, I have an occasional dream that I am floating and being pulled up into a bright white light. I usually wake with a start and can almost feel myself crash landing back in my bed. I don't know what this signifies, if anything. What I do know is that there are a lot of unexplained things that happen in the world every day, and the Cherokee Trace plays host to its fair share of those things.

The Cherokee Trace has been broken, segmented and re-titled in many areas today, but you can still find long stretches of it near Tyler, Gilmer, Nacogdoches, and other towns in East Texas.

The Spirits of Camp Ford

Incredibly, many of the folks who have lived in Tyler their entire lives have no idea that a very important part of Civil War history lies just at the edge of town. I have taken many people there and over ninety percent of them have told me that they had never heard of it before. When I tell them it was one of the largest Civil War prison camps to have existed in that time period, they all seem shocked that it has not received more attention. I believe that the reason it has not been visited more by historians is because it did not have the history of horror attached to it that other prisoner of war camps, such as Andersonville, had. There were many deaths there, to be sure, but there were not as many as was common for a camp that at one time held over 5,000 prisoners. Perhaps, this lack of associated death to the camp is the reason it has kind of faded from popular history.

CAMP FORD, TEXAS.

Line drawing of Camp Ford, from Story of 32nd Iowa Infantry, 1896

Wikipedia has this to say about it: "Camp Ford was a prisoner of war camp near Tyler, TX, during the American Civil War. It was the largest Confederate-run prison west of the Mississippi River.

"Established in the spring of 1862 as a training camp for new Confederate recruits, the camp was named for Col. John Salmon Ford, a Texas Ranger and the Superintendent of Conscripts for the State of Texas. The first Union prisoners to arrive at camp Ford in August 1863 included officers captured in Brashear City, Louisiana in June, and included naval personnel captured when the *Queen Of The West* and the *Diana* were seized by the Union Navy. The captives were initially held in the open, but a panic ensued in November 1863 when eight hundred new prisoners threatened a mass breakout. A military stockade enclosing four acres was soon erected.

"With over 2,000 new prisoners taken in Louisiana on April 8-9, 1864, at the battles of Mansfield, and Pleasant Hill, the stockade was quadrupled in size. With more prisoners captured in Arkansas, the prison's population peaked at about 5,000 in July 1864. The population was reduced by exchanges in July and October 1864, and again in February 1865. The last 1,761 prisoners were exchanged on May 22, 1865.

"During the course of the war, the total number of prisoners who passed through the camp was slightly more than 5,500. About 327 prisoners died in captivity, giving the camp a mortality rate of 5.9%, one of the lowest of any Civil War prison. The deceased prisoners were reinterred to the Alexandria National Cemetery (Alexandria, Louisiana) at Pineville, Louisiana, in 1867."

Now, as you may imagine, there was a lot of crazy things going on in the South during the war. And, of course, as it became clear that the South was losing, the craziness increased to what seemed like acts of hysteria and extreme paranoia. Some folks would argue that people, left to their own devices, revert to primal instincts and evil acts, and the actions people took back then were a direct result of this. In my studies, I have found more than one account of cruel acts and irrational dealings going on during the war years. I guess it is no surprise that Tyler had its own fair share of madness while the battles raged all around.

A book titled *Twenty Months in the Dept of the Gulf* by A. G. H. DuGanne published an excerpt from an account of public executions recounted by the 49th Ohio prisoners at Camp Ford. The incident referred to was known as the "Match Plot." The following is pieced together from these soldier's own written words:

"The breaking out of fires in several stores, at Tyler and other places, awakened a suspicion that two merchants from the Northern States, (who had purchased patent matches, which ignited almost spontaneously,) were incendiaries." "The usual senseless hue and cry followed; the traders were thrown into prison; and hundreds of hapless blacks were arrested and tortured – in order to get evidence of the "Yankee Conspiracy." "Free Negros and poor white settlers from the North fell under the ban at once. Scores of the latter were hanged by the mob." "More than a hundred Negros, free and bond, were executed, as I have been informed, on suspicion alone." "Several were burned at the stake." "Thirty white men were lynched, in and about Tyler and Palestine; one of the unfortunate merchants who had introduced the matches undergoing this fate – the other escaping by timely flight." "Blood flowed in all quarters, 'til the enlightened "Regulators," finding no more poor whites to kill or banish, decided that "order reigned" again."

"Burning men and women at the stake is a relic of aboriginal amusement." "A negro was thus executed at Tyler, while our prisoners tarried at Camp Ford." "The occasion furnished a gala-day for all the good people of Smith County, our guards included."

"I heard one day a story of lynch-law executed in our camp neighborhood; my informant being a friendly guard, who, like many others, was Union at heart, although conforming outwardly to rebel service, as a volunteer."

"During the winter, an old lady, living in Van Zandt County, was plundered by a gang of soldiers in Confederate grey, who beat her shamefully, and (as she told the story,) tied her up by her thumbs 'til she disclosed the place where was concealed her specie (some three hundred dollars) and about two thousand dollars in Confederate currency." "It was asserted that Jayhawkers had done this deed, though sober people shook their heads; well knowing that squads of Sibley's men, with some of Richardson's guerillas, and the scattered miscreants of Quantrell's gang, were ranging through these upper counties." "But "black flag" rebels charged the crime, as they would any crime, on Union men – of whom hundreds, former citizens, were fugitives in swamps and timber, hiding from conscript hunters." "It was easy to accuse such outlawed wanderers; so the chase became set after "Union men." Four individuals were speedily run down: one Reed, a former sheriff of Collin County; an aged citizen, McReynolds, or McRunnells, who had been chief-justice of that district; and two young men, Holcombe and Davis." "They were arrested at their homes and dragged to Tyler."

"This was in May, when our prison-numbers, at Camp Ford, had been increased some thousands, after the battle of Mansfield. The rebels were exultant everywhere, but with characteristic cowardice the people of these counties feared an outbreak from so large a body of incarcerated Yankees, and affected to discover insurrectionary plots continually." "Three noble-hearted Texans, who refused to bow the knee to Davis, were imprisoned in our guardhouse at Camp Ford – two brothers, Whitmore, one of whom had been a prominent member of the Legislature, and Rosenbaum, a former attorney-general of the state." "It was the policy of rank Secessionists to fix as many new crimes on the Union men as could be believed, in order that some pretext might be found for general massacre or the enacting of terror laws."

"Hence, when Sheriff Reed and Judge McReynolds were thrown into prison at Tyler, it was decided that they should never go at large again." "So, one May morning, fifty mounted "Regulators" clattered into Tyler, halted at the tavern door, and "liquored round;" held confab with the provost-marshal, galloped up and down the town awhile, and finally drew rein before the prison, with a yell":

"Bring out them Jayhawkers!"

"The doors were opened, and the men delivered up." "A rope being slung about them, they were dragged behind the Lynchers to a piece of timber, scarce half a mile out of Tyler." "There, almost within gun-shot of camps, where fifteen hundred cavalry and infantry were guarding Federal prisoners, these Lynchers began their mockery of a trial." "The first victim pleaded "not guilty."

"You lie, Jim Reed! You're a heap wuss Jayhawker than Gineral Banks!"

"Silence in the coort!" cries Justice Lynch, a bullheaded whiskey-still proprietor." "Keep still, you all, while I fix his flint." "Prisoner, Jim Reed, what have you got to say why you oughtn't to be black-jacked?"

REED. – "I am not guilty. I've been hunted and persecuted for my sentiments ever since the State seceded. I never fought against the State. My house was burned over the heads of my family in the town where I lived, an honest man, and served the country." "I had to fly, by night, with my wife and seven children, to Van Zandt, and they hounded me out of that." "I declare before Heaven that – "

LYNCH, C. J. – Shet up! You know yer an old scoundrel, and yer was three ye'rs in Missouri Penitentiary –

REED – I never was in the State of Missouri.

LYNCH, C. J. – Blast yer, then, yer an old deserter from General McCulloch's army. The papers was found on ye, and yer can't swar 'em down.

REED. – I deny it. I was regularly commissioned by General McCulloch, as an officer. He gave me a position because I preferred to go back to the army rather than be hunted down. I was preparing to join my command when arrested.

LYNCH, C. J. – Yer a skulkin' liar and a thief, Jim Reed, and we've jest had palaver enough out o' yer. I pronounce judgment of the coort. Yer to be hanged at once, 'til yer dead, dead, dead! And Lord have marcy on yer soul!"

"Five minutes after, Sheriff Reed was dangling from an oak-limb above his murderers."

"Judge McReynolds was then dragged forward and reviled by the 'coort' in like manner." "The old man's son, who was one of the rebel soldiers guarding us at Camp Ford, heard about the Lynchers visiting Tyler jail, and, mounting a horse, galloped from his quarters to the town." "He there learned that the ruffians bad taken their prisoners to the woods." "He followed their trail with all the speed he could command, but arrived in time only to find his father swinging on the tree, from which Reed's dead body had been just cut down." "This wretched son was forced to beg the remains of his parent from the assassins; and so great was the terror inspired by the boldness and cruelty of these "Regulators," that young McReynolds was unable to hire a wagon to convey the corpse to Kaufman County, where his family lived."

"Interior of Camp Ford" from *Harper's Weekly*, March 4, 1865

"Young Holcombe – like each of the others – stoutly maintained his innocence, and was hanged with the same noose that had strangled his predecessors; for the ruffians had provided only rope enough to hang a single man; and were obliged to wait until one was dead before proceeding to execute another."

With all this happening in and around Camp Ford, it is easy to see why it might be a place of unrest for the spirits who linger there. I had heard from a few people who did know the camp was there, that strange things happened there at night.

One of the employees at the gas station across the road also confided in me that she had experienced a few things herself. And naturally, having heard these things, I had to check it out for myself. I decided I would have a hunt there, but before I did, I gathered as much information about the previously experienced phenomena as I could.

I interviewed a few of the residents who live near the camp and found out that almost all of them had some sort of unexplained experience associated with the area. Some said they heard what sounded like rifle or musket fire coming from the wooded area in the site. Others have seen floating lights moving through it. And still others have actually seen full bodied apparitions in Civil War era garb moving about in the camp.

The night clerk at the gas station across the road from the prison told me the most shocking story I heard from the nearby places. She told me that more than one of the employees there had seen a man dressed in a confederate soldier uniform walk across the store and go into the back storage room and disappear. Another employee was frightened enough by it that she quit. Most of them refuse to talk about it – they think that if they ignore it perhaps it will go away.

One Christmas, a certain daring employee hung a stocking in honor of this soldier spirit. They had named the ghost "Charlie" and this was the name placed on the stocking. When the store manager found the stocking, she was angry and ordered them to take it down. A few minutes after they complied and took the stocking down, a large box of lids started spilling onto the floor from a high shelf and eventually tumbled off nearly hitting the manager who had ordered the removal of the stocking. It seemed Charlie liked his inclusion in the Christmas festivities and did not appreciate being excommunicated.

In 2007, a group of paranormal investigators invited me to go investigate the camp one night. I accepted the invitation and arrived around 10PM fully geared up and ready to go. We discovered right away that the investigation was going to be hampered by the close proximity of the highway. The traffic made so much noise we knew it would be hard to catch a decent EVP.

With this in mind, we decided to focus on trying to capture photographic evidence for the first couple of hours. We figured the traffic would die down after midnight and we would have a better chance of capturing sounds. Of the hundreds of pictures we took that night, we ended up with about fourteen that we could not explain. Several had intense orbs and/or weird lights in the woods. One or two had unidentifiable shadows in human shapes. But four of the pictures really got my attention.

In these particular pictures that were taken with a digital camera just seconds apart, a mist is seen rising from the ground, forming first what looks like a man on a horse, then a skeletal face that charges at the camera and displayed such detail as to be able to see pupils in the eyes and teeth in its mouth. You can almost make a flip book of this short series of snap shots. It appears rising, it charges, it grins/screams at the camera, and then passes through us. It gave me goosebumps then, and still does to this day.

When traffic finally died down, we were able to capture one stunning EVP. One of our group heard something. We felt the temperature drop a bit, and a few of us began to feel uneasy. The lady who was trying to capture something on our recording device sensed this and began asking who was with us. She asked: "What is your name?" and low but very distinct, a man's voice answers in a whisper... "Henry." It was the only good EVP we captured that night, but it was enough to make a believer out of me.

A few years later, in 2012, I was giving a tour of the camp to some friends of mine. I was telling them about the historic significance of it and lamenting the lack of funds going into its care. They were a group of historians and paranormal enthusiasts and they all had brought cameras, and one had even brought a video camera. We walked over most of the grounds, including going far back into the wooded area, taking pictures and video the entire way. When we made our way back toward the front of the site, one of the men who was with me asked me to take a look at a picture he had gotten in the doorway of the smaller cabin that sits out in the park.

In the upper right hand corner of the cabin doorway, there was a man's face looking back out at us. There was just a head, with no body to support it floating there. It had sort of freaked the fellow out, as he was definitely not into anything paranormal. He had come along for the history and was shocked at what he had captured. At my request, he sent the picture to my cell phone and then promptly deleted it off his own, wanting absolutely no part of it at all.

A few weeks later, one of the women who had gone with me, specifically the one who was videotaping everything, asked to meet with me. She said she had something to show me. We met the next day and I noticed she had brought her video camera with her. She was grinning from ear to ear and the first words out of her mouth were "You're not going to believe this." Whenever I hear that particular phrase I get excited because I know I'm about to see or hear something very interesting.

As we sat side by side, she turned on her camera and explained she had captured something it took her a while to believe. When we had gone in one of the cabins on the camp site she had been filming, and as she pushed 'play' I saw what had her so jazzed up. Three of us were in the cabin, talking about history and things, and suddenly a fourth person walks through us and right through the cabin wall. You first noticed a fuzzy image, and then it became crystal clear. It was a man, in uniform, walking through us and the wall as if none of us existed. To merely say that I was stunned would be an understatement. It was probably the best video evidence I had ever seen.

Taking into account all that I have experienced at the historic site of Camp Ford, I feel confident saying there is definitely more going on there than meets the eye. Whether there is or not, if you decide to visit, remember the men who were held there. Remember the men who fought for what they believed on both sides of the war, regardless of who was right or wrong. And if you feel so moved, make a donation to the Smith County Historic Society and designate it towards the upkeep of this very important historic site. They operate on a budget, so any donations would be appreciated, and will help to preserve this place for future generations.

The Camp Ford Historic Park is located on US Highway 271, 0.8 miles outside Loop 323 in Tyler, Texas. It is open daily, dawn to dusk, and admission is free. The park features a kiosk with extensive graphics detailing the history of the camp, a walking trail with more interpretive signage, a picnic area, and a reconstruction of two prisoner cabins. There are no restroom facilities, and please understand that portions of the park are not handicap accessible because of the nature of the terrain.

Spirit Halloween Super Store

I find it profoundly ironic that the local Halloween costume shop known as the Spirit Halloween Super Store of Tyler is haunted. It is one of my favorite stores in town and I practically live there during October. The store has been in business for many years and up until the last couple of years it floated around and reappeared each year in a new location. It finally found a permanent home when owners Steve and Charlotte Gomez came upon an old furniture store that had gone out of business. The building is deceptively positioned so as not to appear very large, but once inside you see it is very deep and has a second story with lots of nooks and crannies.

More than one employee mentioned to me that there was definitely something not right about the old building the store now called home. They whispered to me that they had seen shadow figures moving around upstairs and in the back room. One employee told me she had seen a man walk up the stairs and disappear. All of them mentioned the creepy feeling they got in the far rear upstairs storage area. They said it felt like someone was watching you there... like someone was just behind you... about to touch you... but when you turned around no one was there. It was also reported that there were many unidentified noises and voices in the storeroom. And of course, it was downright freaky the way the motion activated toys and novelties would go off of their own accord when no one was anywhere near them.

Being friends with Steve and Charlotte, I asked if they would let me do an investigation there in their off-season, and they were intrigued by the idea. Steve agreed to allow me to bring a crew and spend the night there and even volunteered to stay all night with us. We picked a date and the stage was set.

On the designated night, we came and set up our night vision DVR cameras and spread out with all our equipment and set about finding whatever we could lurking about the old building. The first couple of hours were fairly uneventful, but after midnight it began to get very interesting. We started to capture some strangely-moving, glowing orbs on film, and then there was an unexplainable shadow or two. Before long we began to hear noises that were unidentifiable. We started to experience cold spots and the feeling that we were being watched.

As dead time (3AM) neared, a group of us went upstairs to the rear store room. We were completely in the dark and once we got our bearings, we began to try to instigate something to cause the unseen entity to reveal itself.

At one point I was standing near the outer wall and was overcome with the sensation that something was sneaking up behind me. I whirled around and caught a glimpse of a shadow that was darker than the others around me as it darted down the staircase. I don't know what it was, but it gave me the chills and I felt like it wanted to frighten me away.

We gathered in the center of the room and tried various techniques to get a reaction out of the spirits; we were rewarded with cold touches and whispered threats. We audibly heard a man tell us to get out and caught an EVP of a terrible-sounding laugh. I felt fingers running through my hair and had to restrain myself to keep from running away and probably hurting myself in the dark.

After numerous weird noises and strange sensations, I began to feel like whatever was there really did not like me. I started calling it by every foul name I could think of, saying the most rude, crude, and vulgar things I could conjure to try to get it to lash out at me. The anger and heaviness was palpable, but it didn't do anything more than dart across the room in the shadows and make more strange noises. It was at this point, out of frustration, I must have lost my mind. I suggested the team go downstairs and watch me on the video monitor, leaving me alone in the dark with only an EVP recorder.

Almost immediately I regretted the decision. The noises intensified. The feeling of unease was so strong that I sat down in the middle of the floor in order to make it harder for myself to flee. I began the EVP session by stating I was alone in the dark and wanted to communicate with the "wimpy-ass spirit that was too scared to show itself to the group." Looking back, I think that might have been a poor choice of words.

Something touched me on the arm and it was so cold, my body involuntarily shivered dramatically. Choking back a scream, I ordered it to back off and show itself. That's when my teammate, Brandy, started yelling up the stairs that something was manifesting in the dark in front of me. She said it was big and dark, and was messing with the cameras. She voiced her concern that they might not be able to see me if something happened. About that time I heard something heavy moving in the darkness beside me. I couldn't see what it was, but I could tell it was coming closer.

I'm not ashamed to say that I lost my nerve. I leapt to my feet with astonishing speed for a large fellow, and moved as fast as a man in the dark could toward the staircase and Brandy's voice. The noises kept going behind me and I felt like any minute a hand was going to come from the shadows, clamp down on my shoulder, and pull me back into the void.

I practically flew down the stairs and didn't stop until I was in the middle of the team and bathed in the glow of the video monitors. They tried to explain to me what they saw and I tried to relate what I heard and felt. We all decided it was a good time to call it a night and get the lights back on. Almost comically, we all watched over our shoulders with bad cases of the jitters as we packed up and headed for the door. We were all stoked to have had such an electrifying experience and couldn't wait to review all the evidence.

Incredibly, most of our video and sound were somehow destroyed. When we went to watch it, it seemed the DVR had malfunctioned. We had the first few minutes of footage and the last few seconds and everything in between had been erased. There was unexplainable static on most of the EVP recorders, but we did manage to capture some of the strange sounds and the previously mentioned voices. Everything my recorder had captured while I was upstairs alone was erased. We had almost nothing to show for our night in the Spirit store, except our personal experiences and memories. It seemed that whatever is there did not want us to expose it.

All I can say for certain is that there is definitely a spirit of some sort in the old building and it definitely does not like me. And that, my friends, is exactly why I intend to go back and try it again.

Spirit Halloween Super Store is open from late September until the first of November and is located at 3717 S. Broadway Ave (across from Pep Boys) in Tyler, Texas. During the off-season, the building doubles as a shop full of antiques, oddities, and some of the strangest things you may ever see. And it is rumored that owners, Steve and Charlotte, intend to begin having murder mystery dinners and other events in partnership with Tours of Tyler... so keep an eye on them to learn more!

The Old Smith County Jail

One of the most interesting places that I've ever visited on my quest for all things paranormal was the old Smith County Jail. I had heard many stories about the people who died there and the crazy instances of wrongful imprisonment, and I knew if I ever got the opportunity I was certainly going to investigate there. As luck would have it, I got my chance one summer night after convincing my friend, and current owner of the historic building, Mr. Randy Gilbert, to let me have a crack at it.

To begin with, let me tell you a little about the history of the place. Houston architect Eugene T. Heiner and builder Henry Kane designed and built this structure in 1881 to serve as Smith County's fourth jail. An 1894 second-story addition doubled the jail's cell space. The building was replaced by a new jail in 1916. It then became the Lewis Hotel until 1986. It features classical detailing of the Italianate style, a stucco finish scored to look like cut stone, elaborate window molds and consoles, and classical beltcourses. It was recorded as a Texas Historic Landmark in 1993.

One of the most intriguing features of the jail is that it has an outside holding cell. Mr. Gilbert explained that the cell was exactly like the cells that would have been in the building during its official use. Seeing it set outside, reminds one of how some treatment of prisoners could be a bit inhumane before current regulations were put in place. The cells are tiny and if any more than one person was placed in them, there would barely be space to breathe. Previous inmates had scratched their names all over the walls of these outdoor cells.

And after much research, we were able to find out a bit about the most prominent name on the wall. Mr. Fritz Braatz was a German immigrant who got himself thrown in the pokey many years back. Evidently he got a little too drunk during a night out with the boys. The records showed he went on to have a family in Waco, Texas and did pretty good for himself. Perhaps the tiny, humiliating cell did him some good.

Mr. Gilbert told us stories of shoot outs in the jail and public hangings that had taken place there. One was truly tragic as the man in question had been accused of rape and was taken out of jail by an angry mob and hung outside. Then just a couple of hours after he was hung, the accusing lady came forth and admitted she had made the whole thing up because she was angry. But of course, nothing was done to her. I imagine those involved in the hanging just wanted to disassociate themselves from the nasty business.

I began my evening in the jail by setting up my hunting equipment with my team of investigators and exploring every nook and cranny with a psychic friend. She told me where she felt the hot spots and where she thought I was most likely to get some interesting activity. As the night progressed, we found out she was very right.

It wasn't long before our DVR cameras began detecting movement in empty rooms and our EMF readers began going off where they had not just moments before. And when we broke out the spirit box, we began communicating with a spirit that seemed to really like one of the ladies who was investigating with us. This spirit told us that she looked like his wife and he missed her cooking. Now, this lady, being a professional ghost hunter with the Carthage, Texas based group, the Paranormal Junkies, was used to getting interesting communications from beyond, but she was a bit shocked to hear there was a spirit infatuated with her. At one point the temperature dropped around her several degrees, the EMF reader began going off and she felt as if she were being touched.

Another of the group was with me in a smaller room on the second story when we both began experiencing strange happenings. Our psychic friend had told us she sensed a female spirit in this area who was hiding in the corner as if she had been hurt. The lady who went in the room with me was also a talented psychic and she agreed there was definitely something in the corner. When we got over there, our detectors started going off and our periscope lit up several times. We both began to feel agitated and we developed headaches. The more we tried to communicate, the worse the headache became until we had to leave the room. As we went down the staircase, one of our members was pushed by an unseen force in the middle of her back and if we hadn't caught her, she would have taken a nasty tumble down the stairs.

As the night progressed, more and more things began to happen. We were catching movement much more frequently on our DVR cameras and we had captured a few EVPs. We decided to spend the 3AM hour upstairs in a large room that we had gotten strong EMF readings in earlier...the same room where we had communicated with the spirit who missed his wife's cooking.

It started slow, but sure enough we started getting hits on the readers and the spirit box started squawking again. A new spirit came through and he wasn't pleasant. He said he died wrongly and was not at peace. He made the temperature of the room drop considerably and he kicked one of our members in the leg. She yelped in pain and stood up from her chair quickly. This angered me so I told the spirit to pick on me and not her. It obliged.

I was sitting in an office chair that rolled and I began to feel the chair trying to move with me in it. I called this to everyone's attention and they watched the chair move under its own power. One of the group brought the EMF reader over and placed it on my shoulder and it started going off. I began to feel the chair rocking. Everyone gasped because they saw it too. I told the spirit in a stern voice to stop playing around and if it was going to move me it should go ahead and move me across the room. At this point, we caught one of the clearest class 'A' EVPs I have ever heard.

A man's voice was on the recorder when we played it back asking: "Is he pissed off?" right after I demanded to stop being toyed with. It was as clear as if the person speaking it had been standing and holding the recorder. I was a bit stunned.

We began feeling uneasy and decided it was time to wrap up our investigation, so we packed up our equipment and started to leave. As we walked out the door, one of the other hunters came to me and informed me that our psychic had left before we went upstairs and said she was not feeling good being in there and that someone was going to get hurt. Now I was really stunned. She left before we got kicked and shoved, and as I watched the lady who got kicked limp to her car, I knew our psychic had been right. I made a mental note to ask her to relay messages like that to me directly next time. I might have ended the investigation early had I known. OK, probably not...but maybe!

The old Smith County Jail is currently owned by Mr. Randy Gilbert who uses it as his base of operations for his law office. It is located on Erwin Street between the Smith County Courthouse and United States Highway 271.

The Goodman LeGrand Mansion

The Goodman LeGrand Mansion and museum is an amazing place in Tyler. This fine, old home stands out as a beautiful testament to days gone by. I have been lucky enough to visit the house on many occasions and have become friends with the curator, Mrs. Patricia Heaton. She has gone above and beyond in the upkeep and restoration of the home and is a wonderful person to know. The history of the home is a long and interesting one and the following excerpts were taken directly from the advertising rack cards that Patricia uses to promote tourism of the museum:

"The Goodman home was originally built in 1859 as a one-story, four-room house, and it was established on a 9-acre wooded parcel of land. It was known as Bonnie Castle by its first owner and occupant, Samuel Gallatin Smith. The young well-to-do bachelor and attorney sold the house in 1861 when the Civil War broke out. Mr. Smith became a Captain in the Confederacy and was later killed in battle in Louisiana. The next owner who bought the home in 1861 was Franklin N. Gary, a local school teacher. In 1866, a year after the Civil War ended, Dr. Samuel Adams Goodman, a retired country doctor from South Carolina, purchased the house from Mr. Gary. The following year in 1867, his son, Dr. William Jeffries Goodman, a local doctor and Civil War Major and Chief Surgeon, bought the house from his father and moved in with his new bride, Mary Priscilla Gaston. Her brother was William Henry Gaston, a founder of the city of Dallas, and one of Dallas' first millionaires. For 73 years and four generations, this prominent family made the house their family home.

Dr. & Mrs. W.J. Goodman raised three children in the home. They added the second story to the house, in the Italianate-style architecture, around 1880 in order to accommodate their growing family. Their oldest child and daughter, Sallie Gertrude Goodman, married James H. LeGrand in October, 1893. She and her husband lived here throughout their lives, and after the deaths of Sallie's parents, siblings, and her 2 year old son who died in 1896. In 1926, Sallie and her husband, James, remodeled the house to its current state, which is in the Classic Revival-style architecture. The 1926 remodel included the construction of the projecting circular porticos and the massive 2-story columns that the Goodman is so well known for today. When Sallie Goodman LeGrand died in 1939, four years after her husband's death, she was the last direct heir to live in the house. Upon her death, she bequeathed the Goodman-LeGrand estate (the land, home and furnishings) to the City of Tyler, with instructions to maintain the historic family home and to keep it open as a public museum. The City of Tyler officially took ownership in 1940. Much of what we currently know about the home and its past residents comes from journals kept by Sallie. Her diaries recount tales about guests who stayed in the house to escape the dangers of the Civil War, stories of the numerous family trips, and where a lot of the furnishings and artifacts originally came from. The journals also describe several elegant social galas that took place in the home, supper parties and receptions held for Texas state politicians.

The Goodman-LeGrand at night

In 2010-2011, the Goodman-LeGrand underwent a major exterior renovations project, which brought the exterior paint and shingled mansard roof back to its original colors from the 1880 remodel. Today, the home is still furnished with the original belongings of the Goodman-LeGrand family, some of which are older than the house itself as they date back to the early 1800s. The museum offers visitors a chance to view such items as antique hand carved furniture and musical instruments, a grandfather clock from the colonial era, fine silver and crystal, hand-painted Limoges china, original clothing, medical books dating back to the early 1800s, Civil War-era surgical tools and medical cases, original paintings and photographs, and many other rare and interesting items. Step back in time and see what makes the Goodman unique!"

There are many stories that circulate around Smith County about the hauntings going on in the mansion. I was lucky enough to hear some of these stories directly from the people who experienced them.

It seems that back during the late 1960s there was a young curator who lived in the home in a small room upstairs room. It seemed easier, I'm sure, to be on the property at all times to oversee all work being done and to be ready for tours and events at a moment's notice. And it did work for a while. Then the noises started.

One night the curator heard noises coming from downstairs that sounded like the tinkling of glass, the laughter of many people, and piano music. He immediately called the police, assuming someone had broken in. Of course when the police arrived they found nothing and assumed the young man was hearing things. It was dismissed as a bad dream and left at that.

However, it happened again a few nights later, and again a few nights after that. Each time the police arrived they dismissed it as over active imagination and finally asked that they not be called again unless there was proof of a break in. Facing this ultimatum, the man decided to handle things on his own.

The next time the noises started, he got out of his bed and stealthily eased into the upstairs hallway and down the staircase. He was halfway down the stairs when he met a man dressed in turn of the century attire coming up the stairs. The Victorian gentleman was carrying a wine glass and seemed startled to see the young curator on the staircase. Without missing a beat, the party-goer tilted his head quizzically and asked the curator: "Why don't you join the party?" and then vanished right in front of his eyes. Needless to say, the curator was scared out of his wits and resigned shortly after he finished cleaning his under garments.

A few years later, a couple men were hired to work on the house after hours. They were steadily working on the trim work downstairs one night when one of them decided he was hungry and offered to go get food for the both of them. After he left the other man continued his duties.

It wasn't long before he began to hear piano music coming from upstairs. He didn't know what to make of it and stood silently listening for a long time. He finally decided to go investigate. Halfway up the staircase, he met a beautiful lady in a white, Victorian ball gown coming down the stairs. He asked her who she was and what she was doing in the house. He told her it was after hours, the museum was closed and she would have to leave. She leaned forward, smiled at him, let out a laugh and vanished before his eyes.

When his friend came back with lunch, he was sitting beside the front gate refusing to go back inside. According to the fellow who told me this story, it was the last time and work was done in the home over night. Later on, he said that he was sure the lady on the stairs was Etta... Sallie Goodman's sister who died at a young age.

Flashing forward several years after Patricia had taken over as curator of the museum, another strange thing happened. Patricia's assistant, had come to work early one day and as she parked and got out of her car, she looked up in the upstairs window because something caught her eye. She noticed a woman up in the bedroom, combing her long brown hair. Patricia has long brown hair, so the assistant assumed it was she up there for whatever reason brushing her hair.

When the assistant went to open the door and announce her presence, she noticed Patricia's car was not there...and the alarm was still set. She called Patricia's name to see if she would get an answer. There was no reply, but she heard footsteps coming from above her head in the bedroom in question. She didn't go any farther until Patricia arrived.

Moving like the cartoon characters in Scooby Doo, they slowly, stealthily searched the museum and found no one. After this, both the assistant and curator experienced too many things to recount. Patricia is at peace with it, and feels like she has been welcomed into the world of the Goodman's. She just hired a new assistant, however, and new reports are already coming in.

We did manage to have an overnight hunt there and we captured some amazing things. The most interesting things to me were a door closing of its own accord when no one was around, and several EVP's saying Patricia's name in them. I loved my time there and think it is just about the most wonderful place in Tyler.

The staircase at Christmas

The Goodman LeGrand Mansion & Museum is located at 624 N. Broadway Ave. in Tyler, TX and is open for regular tours Tuesday through Saturday from 10AM to 4PM. There is also a rose garden on the grounds and it is featured in the Azalea Trails celebration every spring. The house is owned by the City of Tyler and is available for rentals for events and weddings. For more information, give them a call at 903-531-1286.

The Liberty Theater

A friend of mine operates the recently restored Liberty Theater in Tyler and she mentioned to me that there were some interesting things going on there. Actors and hosts for various productions had spoken of weird sensations in the green room and feelings of being watched. One or two guests had spotted someone in the balcony when no one was there and on one occasion a lady said she felt like someone was touching her and there was no one nearby. That was enough information for me to gather the gang and spend the night alone inside the classic theater.

The Liberty Theater originally was opened in 1930. It was owned by Mr. and Mrs. Wilbur Shieldes and was operated as a first-run movie theater on the south side of the Tyler square. The very first film to play on its screen was an adventure/romance titled *Blaze of Glory*, which sadly, has no current prints in existence. The theater saw many promotional gimmicks and many movie stars come and go through its doors. Lines stretched around the block when it played *Gone with the Wind*, *Bridge on the River Kwai* and many others through the years. It managed to be a success and continued in operation for 50 years.

The Liberty Theater circa 1990

The Liberty finally became a "discount theater" in the early to mid 1980s and eventually closed its doors around 1986. It sat vacant for many years with a parade of people coming and looking at it with intent to buy, but the only folks that did ante up, gutted the building and destroyed any semblance of the old glory in one fell swoop. Fortunately for us, they ran out of money halfway through their "renovations" and the City of Tyler purchased the building in 2008 for $180,000. Seeing the need for a venue that had a classic, elegant feel and in an attempt to help revitalize the downtown area of Tyler, they subsequently renovated it using donations of over $1 million.

The Liberty Theater circa 2008

The Liberty is once again home to memory-making events and entertainment, including screenings of classic films, after it was converted into Liberty Hall and re-opened in September 2011. It was an amazing blast from the past when I went to see the original *Terminator* movie there... like a trip back through time.

On the night of our investigation, we were all a bit giddy. It was sort of like a child's dream to have an entire movie theater to play around in. But once the lights went out and the investigation began in earnest, our giddiness was replaced fairly quickly with a sense of foreboding due to one of our party feeling a presence in the green room as soon as she entered.

She told me she first felt coldness on her shoulder followed by a groping sensation on her thigh. Her EMF reader began to go off when she held it near her leg. Another investigator who was in the room saw a shadowy figure back away from her when she asked it to stop, and move into a small dressing room. He followed the shadow into the room and witnessed it move right through a wall and disappear.

Later on in the night, myself and two others were in the same room and our equipment suddenly started going off and once again the female who was with us felt something cold touching her on her legs and lower back. It didn't stop on her thighs and she became very uncomfortable and asked to leave the room. As soon as she left, our equipment became silent and we experienced nothing else in there. Whatever spirit haunts that space seemingly enjoys female company much more than male.

A lone investigator in the back stage area, behind the screen and the curtains, captured an EVP of a man's voice saying simply "hello... hello... hello." Another one of us caught a photo of an unexplained shadow in human shape in the same area.

The most amazing thing that happened that night came at around 2:30 in the morning. We had gathered in the auditorium and were discussing the areas we wanted to cover during the quickly approaching dead time and we heard someone walking up in the balcony. We quickly did a head count and yes, we were all present and accounted for...but the sounds continued.

Two of our party had cameras at the ready and began taking pictures of the balcony area as fast as they could. I and two others ran up the stairs to see if we could figure out where the sounds were coming from. As soon as we reached the upper level, the sounds stopped...but our equipment was going off. We began taking pictures and checking in every nook and cranny, because we half thought someone was really there messing with us. We found nothing, but the pictures told a different story.

Once we were satisfied that no one was there and the equipment settled down, we gathered in the auditorium again. It was at this point that our lead tech member let out a gasp and showed us her picture. It was amazing. Almost as clear as day, you could see a man standing in the balcony wearing blue jeans, a checked shirt, and a cowboy hat. It was as if he had posed for the picture but it had come out a little blurry. A second picture, captured by another member showed a bright orb near the same location. And our recorder caught some strange mumbled noises that sounded like human speech but could not be made clear.

Interior of Liberty Hall circa 2013

As the night ended, we determined there was something definitely in the theater that was of ethereal nature, but we had no idea who it could be or why it was there. We hope to get back into the theater for another night soon and try to solve the mystery of the "cowboy ghost."

The Liberty Theater, now known as Liberty Hall is located at 103 E. Erwin St in Tyler, TX and has regularly scheduled events. To find out more about Liberty Hall, visit them online at www.libertytyler.com .

The Barron-Shackelford & New Bethel (Werewolf Road) Cemeteries

Every town seems to have that one special place where high school age kids go to scare one another and generally cause mischief. This cemetery is that place for Tyler kids. It's an odd place to be sure. There is an almost-forgotten cemetery on one side of a fence with just a few graves scattered throughout it dating back to the 1800s. Just on the North West side of that fence is the New Bethel Cemetery more commonly known as "Werewolf Road Cemetery."

The Bethel side has graves dating back to the 1940s and is still in use, though rarely, to this day. It is located on a sloping piece of ground that is terribly rocky and filled with red clay. It does not seem to be the most ideal place for a graveyard to be located.

The road it is on is just a county road, but throughout the years, it has been told that ghosts and werewolves haunt this area and so everyone knows it as "Werewolf Road." Many a high school male has taken their sweethearts out there in the middle of the night and pretended the car stalled and turned off the lights. Then the ghost stories begin until the poor girl is (hopefully) squeezed up as tightly as she can get to the storyteller.

Entrance to New Bethel (Werewolf Road) Cemetery

Of course with every legend, there is some truth. This one is no exception. The stories began back during the early 1900s when a young couple was supposedly found gibbering and crying that they had faced down a werewolf out there and had barely escaped with their lives. And more was added to the lore when supposedly a person's car was shaken violently from side to side while sitting out there one night.

Inside New Bethel (Werewolf Road) Cemetery

There have been multiple retellings of these stories and many folks swear that your car will be shaken if you sit there quietly in the dark. It seems the best time for this to happen is around 2 in the morning. I personally have met more than twenty people who say it happened to them. Some folks say they are too frightened to even go out there after dark.

I decided it was a place worth looking into and began to do some research. I discovered that the Bethel cemetery is an African American cemetery and may have been started on the other side of that separating fence due to segregation. The smaller, older cemetery on the other side of that fence is known as the Barron-Shackleford Cemetery and seems to have a lot of children and young folks buried there.

Somewhere in the 1980s a few people were caught doing strange things out there including witchcraft and Satanism. There are still remnants of black, melted wax on some of the tombs and a mostly faded pentagram. I also discovered that one

139

time someone had done some grave robbing out there and some of the burial sites are caving in. With all these unnatural acts being committed there, it is easy to see why some spirits may have been disturbed.

Car waiting to be "shaken by ghosts" at
New Bethel (Werewolf Road) Cemetery

When I finally decided to investigate the area, I chose to bring a psychic with me. I asked my friend, Mike McCaskill, to make the journey with me as he is one of the most accurate, sensitives (psychics) I know. He agreed and we set out on our way, with Mike being the only equipment we brought along. Often, he is more than enough and he proved himself once again when we arrived.

We hadn't been out of the car very long before we all heard footsteps in the grass nearby and a man's voice mumbling in the dark. Sufficiently spooked, we headed deeper into the graves and Mike began communicating with someone none of the rest of us could see. He told us that most of the spirits had sort of given up on the place and moved on but there were a few still remaining. He confirmed everything I had heard about the place and told me that the spirits were irritated that we were even there.

He was in the midst of explaining to me that these remaining spirits considered themselves guardians when he stopped cold and put his arms out in a signal for us to stop moving and be quiet. We were near the fence that separates the two graveyards when this happened and we all stood silently for what seemed liked forever.

Mike suddenly turned to us and said we should go. I was a bit stunned. There isn't much that bothers Mike and I had never seen him have this reaction. I questioned him as to how serious he was and he replied: "Dude, let's put it this way... I'm leaving... you can stay if you want, but I wouldn't recommend it." And he headed back toward the car. We followed but I kept questioning what could be so bad as to make him want to leave so suddenly. After all, other than a few things I had heard on investigations before, I had heard nor seen a thing to make me want to run.

He talked as he walked and explained to me that there was something out there that was not human and never had been. He said that something had been "called up" at some point or another during the rituals that had been held there and it had taken an interest in us... more specifically...in him. He said it felt like some sort of "elemental" and in his words it was "nasty" and "foul."

As we reached the car and wasted no time getting inside, he continued, saying that whatever it was is confined there and thought Mike might be its ticket out. He said he got the feeling it was just plain evil and should be left alone. And with that, we left and have not discussed it since.

The Barron (Shakelford) & New Bethel Cemeteries are located directly south of Tyler, Texas. From Tyler, take US69S to the intersection of CR2813 and turn left (east). This cemetery is about 1.5 miles along CR2813 and is on the north side of the road.

Tyler Civic Theatre

The city has a true treasure in the Tyler Civic Theatre. It began as a little troop of actors performing at the local high school in 1927 and changed locations three times over the years as it grew. It finally ended up over near the famous Rose Garden and fair grounds. It was unique in that it was designed to be a theatre in the round...meaning there is no back stage area and the audience literally encircles the action.

It wasn't long before they realized they needed more space. Almost every show sold out for every performance and the season ticket holders held most of the seats. Through friends of the theater and lots of great people, enough money was raised to build a second, bigger auditorium next door with almost double the capacity of the first. Keeping with tradition, the second auditorium is also a theatre in the round but with comfortable stadium style seating all the way around it. Now, it is possible to perform two plays simultaneously.

143

The older theatre is mostly used for children's performances and special events. It has been dubbed the "Rogers Children's Theatre." The newer, bigger theatre is used for the adult plays and also special events and has been named the "Braithwaite Theatre." There are performances and acting classes and amazing shows held all year long and it is definitely worth checking out. In fact, it has been said that the performances here are every bit as good as anything you might see in Dallas or other larger cities. And, it should be noted that it is the longest, continuously running, theatre in the round in the USA.

I love theatres. I always have. And I seem to be drawn to them. No matter where I end up, if I stay for any length of time, I end up in the theatre for one reason or another. My first experience with this one was as a volunteer usher and concession attendant. I enjoyed it very much and came back often. Of course, with frequent trips, I became acquainted with a lot of the staff and the other volunteers and of course, many of the actors. And it did not take long to begin hearing stories of the ghost that haunts the place. I wasn't surprised to hear it; after all, any theatre worth its salt ought to have a theatre ghost.

One day I cornered one of the staff and asked her to tell me what had been experienced there and to walk me around while we talked. She agreed after giving me a curious look as if to say: What are you up to? I confessed I was a ghost hunter and was fascinated by the paranormal. She seemed amused and began to lead me through the place as she talked. We went into all the nooks and crannies of the place as she described what she had experienced and what she had been told. I enjoyed it very much.

What I learned that day was that there was a male spirit inhabiting the building and that he had been a long time, and much beloved, director and manager there in years gone by. He was meticulous and exacting and he was generous and kind. He made the theater run smoothly and put on phenomenal shows.

144

But one thing he didn't do was put up with prima donnas and actors who didn't learn their lines.

Almost immediately after he left this world, strange things started happening at the theatre...mostly happening in the Rogers Theatre side of the building as that was the side he knew in life. When an actor gets out of hand and becomes full of himself, he finds ways to put them back in their place. He will make the spot light on them go off in the middle of their scene and come back on after. He will hide their things in the dressing rooms and he will find numerous other ways to let them know of his displeasure.

Conversely, if he is happy with a performance, he will make the light shining on his favorites flicker rhythmically as if he is clapping for them. Footsteps have been heard when no one is around, and a man has been spotted sitting in the shadows of the auditoriums but is not really there when the lights are put on the spot. Sometimes the props can't be found but magically turn up in time for the performance...as if he went and found it and brought it to where it was needed.

Everyone I talked to seemed to love their theatre ghost and enjoyed his watchful eye on them. I was tickled over the antics they described and I dubbed him the "persnickety theatre ghost." And from then on, I kept an eye out for him every time I came to work a show or visit.

When I was looking for a place to host my annual Paranormal Conference that I have every spring, I immediately thought of the Civic Theatre. After making arrangements to host it there, I took a few of my friends and assistants through and was giving them a tour of the place as we laid out where everything would take place. We had entered the Rogers Theatre auditorium and I had just turned on the lights so we could see it when I began explaining what was going to happen there. I spoke out loud on the topics of the paranormal that would be discussed.

Suddenly, one of my helpers asked if anyone else had noticed that it looked like a man was sitting in the corner when we entered. Two others agreed they had seen it too, but I had been focused on getting the lights on and had missed it. About that time, I said that I hoped the theatre ghost approved of what we were doing on his stage and almost instantly, the spotlight that was shining on us got a bit brighter and started flickering rhythmically. I remembered what I had been told about the "clapping effect" and I smiled. The others with me had startled looks on their faces and were trying to figure out who was in the light booth. One of them even swore she saw a man in there. I just laughed and told them I thought we had approval to carry on and so we did...as I relayed to them the ghost story.

Sure enough, the conference went off without a hitch and was said to be the best one several of the speakers and guests had ever attended. For that, I thank that persnickety ghost and I plan on continuing to host the event there for as long as it can contain it. It's a wonderful place and he is one spirit I like having around. So if you go there, be prepared to be blown away by the caliber of the performances, but keep a watchful eye for my ghostly friend, and maybe he will say hello.

The Tyler Civic Theatre is located at 400 Rose Park Drive, next to the Rose Garden in Tyler, Texas. Their performance schedule can be found by going to their web site at www.tylercivictheatre.com.

Roseland Plantation

Roseland, Ben Wheeler, Texas

Roseland Plantation is an antebellum plantation house located five miles east of Edom in southeast Van Zandt County near Tyler. Burwell H. Hambrick, who moved to Texas from Virginia, purchased a 500-acre tract from Thomas R. Buford on April 9, 1852. He later purchased an additional 2,500 acres. Shortly thereafter, Hambrick set to building his dream home. Construction on the two-story Greek Revival house, erected near the site of a Cherokee battle of 1839, was completed by 1854. The house is made of wood with pegged mortise and tenon construction. Bricks for the fireplaces and foundation were made by hand on the plantation. Hambrick also built a church and a private racetrack nearby.

The house, located halfway between Dallas and Shreveport, served at times as a stagecoach stop and a change station for horses. In early years it also served as an area social center. After the Civil War, Hambrick deeded much of the property to his former slaves, and part of the plantation land became the foundation for the Red Land High School and community. In 1868 Hambrick formed a partnership with George Humphrey to establish a cotton-thread mill in Tyler. The mill burned in 1869, and Hambrick, reduced to poverty, died a year later. Another gentleman stepped in and bought the property shortly thereafter.

William S. Herndon held title to the house until 1919, after which the house sat vacant until the 1950s. In 1954 Mrs. W. C. Windsor, wife of a Tyler oilman, found the house abandoned and collapsing in upon itself. She fell in love with it and bought it, along with 200 acres, renamed it Roseland, and restored it... at great expense. By the time she found it, it had fallen into such disrepair that the chimney had fallen, the columns had fallen, and there were gaping holes in the walls. Her tireless efforts have made it a beautiful place to visit. It is currently owned by Tim and Carolyn West who revere its history and beauty and intend to keep it in the best of shape.

In 1966 the Texas Historical Commission placed a marker on the site. Various stories and legends are associated with the house. The upper east bedroom is said to have been the scene of the murder of a young girl, and spectral horsemen are rumored to visit the building... perhaps remembering it as a stopping point on their endless travels. The historical marker indicates the place where, according to local lore, the groans of Cherokee Chief Bowles, who died in the battle of 1839 on the property, can be heard. In the 1880s, a thief identified as Peter Hill is said to have taken baskets of gold from the house.

It was these stories and legends that drew me to the house. After meeting with Tim and Carolyn, I found out more of the depth of the legends. It turned out that the girl who died in the upstairs bedroom was not murdered, but rather committed suicide. She was heartbroken over her lover going to war and never returning. There have been countless reports of the young lady appearing in the upstairs window holding a candle. She wanders across the upstairs balcony and wails a great lament and vanishes. You can imagine what a sight this must have been to passerby during the time the house was falling down and abandoned. Tim said their guests had experienced seeing the girl when they stay in that particular bedroom. He said he wished they knew how to help her rest in peace.

The haunted bedroom at Roseland

The ghostly horsemen always come at night and often visit the chapel located beside and behind the main house. It is supposed to sound like two or three horses being ridden hard and then stopping suddenly. There are whinnies and snorts from the horses and men commanding in harsh voices and then it is all gone as quickly as it begins.

Other strange knocks and sounds have been heard throughout the property and some things just do not seem to have a logical explanation. Many folks who live nearby have a fondness for the old home but also a certain wary respect for the spirits within. Almost everyone I spoke with said they loved the home and thought it was beautiful but none of them would ever spend the night there.

Of course I was intrigued by the place and after discussing the time and date with Tim, was given permission to hunt it. It turned into a long night with one thing after another happening. We caught strange floating orbs and other things on camera. We captured several EVP's that sounded, indeed, like horses…and a few that were voices but only one we could make out. The one we deciphered was a woman or a girl and she was asking "why are you here?" It certainly gave me a chill or two when I heard it on the recorder. We had several personal experiences that included light touches and voices we did not capture on our recorders.

All in all, it was a great night and we captured enough for me to agree that there is definitely a female spirit there and who knows what all else. It was a treat to be allowed the freedom to wander inside and outside on the grounds at night.

There were moments when the sounds of the modern world melted away…when the night noises and the setting itself made it easy to imagine what it must have been like in the 1800s. I hope to go back soon and see what else the elegant home will share with us.

Roseland Plantation Home is located on Highway 64, approximately 24 miles from downtown Canton, Texas, and 13 miles from downtown Tyler, Texas. It sits high up on a majestic hill overlooking the road. The house is open for tours by appointment and is available to book for events. Also, there is an amazing thing in the antique display building. I won't tell you what it is, but make sure you ask to see it if you stop by. It will take your breath away. For more information, check them out online at roselandplantation.com

Monument to a Massacre

The Killough Monument, Jacksonville, Texas

The Killough Monument and cemetery is a reminder of a terrible event in Texas' past. The year was 1837; Sam Houston and the Texan army had defeated Santa Anna at the Battle of San Jacinto, giving Texas independence from Mexico.

Wanting to seek his fortune in the new promised land of the Republic of Texas, Issac Killough, Sr., moved his family from Talladega, Alabama to East Texas. He purchased land that had originally been part of a treaty settlement between the Texas Revolutionary Government and the Cherokee Indians; this settlement had been negotiated by John Forbes, John Cameron and Sam Houston. In December of 1837, however, the Senate of the new nation of Texas nullified the treaty. The Cherokee weren't happy with the treaty because it greatly reduced their lands – since they were led to believe that it would give them a permanent home, however, they accepted the terms. Some bitterness still existed among many tribe members, and the nullification of the treaty only exacerbated those feelings. The stage was set for an inevitable clash between the Texans and the Cherokee.

On Christmas Eve of 1837, Issac Killough didn't know about this rising animosity with the natives. His four sons, two daughters and their husbands, and two single men, Elbert and Barakias Williams had all settled on the land. Over the next several months they built houses, and planted crops to sustain their families.

The corn was ready to harvest by August, but word had reached the settlers of a growing threat by the Indians. The Killough party joined with other settlers and fled to the city of Nacogdoches for safety.

In a month or so, the threat seemed to have dissipated, or so the Killoughs thought. They struck a bargain with the Indians to allow them to return to the land to harvest their crops, promising to leave before the first frost of winter.

Apparently not all of the Cherokees respected the arrangement, however, because on the afternoon of October 5, 1838, a renegade band attacked and killed or kidnapped eighteen unarmed members of the Killough party, including Issac Killough, Sr., himself.

The survivors, which included Issac's wife Urcey, began a harrowing journey to Lacy's Fort, forty miles south of the Killough settlement. When they arrived there safely, an enraged General Thomas J. Rusk organized a militia and rode out in search of the Indians. Rusk's men caught up with them near Frankston, and defeated them in a skirmish in which eleven of the Indians were killed.

The Killough Massacre was the largest Indian depredation in East Texas. The bodies that were found were buried at the site, and in the 1930s the W.P.A. erected an obelisk made of stone to mark the location. In 1965 the cemetery was dedicated as a Texas Historical Landmark, and the area is now enclosed by a fence with a small parking lot beside it.

There are stories scattered across the Internet about the spirit of an Indian in full battle dress appearing on a horse, and a mysterious fog that appears even on warm, sunny days. None of the sites seemed to be all that credible – and by that I mean backed up by investigation – so the Native American specter sounded a lot like an urban legend.

I wanted to visit the site anyway, and it turned out to be an incredibly interesting place.

The graves of the massacre victims at the site

Before I actually visited the monument, I'd heard quite a bit about supernatural activity there, including the aforementioned sighting of a Cherokee warrior and the mysterious fog. Several paranormal investigators who'd been there had regaled me with stories of odd temperature readings, electric fields, and other scientific measurements often associated with ghosts. I wanted to see the place for myself, though, both for the historical aspects, as well as the spirits that might be showing up there.

I drove through Jacksonville, then headed north on highway 69. It wasn't long until I saw a sign that said, "Killough Monument" with an arrow pointing to the west. I followed FM 855 a short distance until I came to an identical sign pointing south to FM 3405. I turned my vehicle in that direction, and started looking for the monument. Almost an hour later, I was still looking for it. There was a maze of little Farm/Market roads and I covered most of them; more than a few times I was sure that I was lost. I even stopped and asked people how to find the Killough Monument, but those few that had even heard of it couldn't tell me where it was. One fellow said, "I'm not sure, but I think it's around here somewhere, though."

I finally gave up, and headed back home. It took a few weeks and quite a bit of research, but I finally found the exact directions, and I followed them on an online map before ever leaving home. If the monument was where they said it was, I'd been all around it on my previous visit, and had even driven past the turn-off road.

Armed with that information, I set out for Jacksonville once again. Sure enough, this time I drove straight to the monument.

I have to say that when you first see it, the stone obelisk is quite impressive – the stone composition has the same look as W.P.A. buildings from the 1930s. The graves of those who were found dead are around its base, and the entire area is surrounded by a fence with a historical marker near the entrance. It was beautifully kept, and on that particular day, very serene.

When I got out of my car I noticed one thing that truly turned my stomach – someone had spray-painted a pentagram on the parking lot. If I live to be a hundred years old, I will still never understand how some people can bring themselves to vandalize property like that... especially at a sacred place such as a cemetery.

I just shook my head, sighed, and continued on. I walked through the gate, and walked around to take a good look at the place. As I walked around inside the fence, a rush of emotion hit me – it was as if I was feeling an overwhelming sense of fear. I think that this was one of the strongest impressions that I've ever had investigating a haunted location. It was literally all that I could do to keep from running back to my car and locking the doors.

There was certainly no rational reason for the feeling. The place seemed to be very safe, and although it was far out in the country, there were many homes within a short distance. I simply couldn't explain the feeling that I was experiencing, and the longer I stayed, the more intense it became.

My scientific side was questioning whether or not my imagination could simply be getting the best of me, but I dismissed that notion immediately. It was too strong a sensation, and try as I wanted, I couldn't get rid of the sense of dread.

As I snapped a few photos, I realized that I'd had as much as I could stand. Something was urging me to get away from there very quickly, so I did. I managed to keep from running, but I did walk rather quickly. I also couldn't help but look back over my shoulder again and again, since I was sure that something was coming for me.

I almost jumped into the car, slammed the door shut, and then hit the electric locks. I felt better, but not *that* much. It wasn't until I was several miles down the road that I was feeling like myself again.

Whether I had been influenced by supernatural forces at the massacre site, or I'd just picked up on the residual feelings from that terrible event, I'll probably never know. I wanted to go back at some point, though, if for no other reasons than to pay my respects to the settlers who are buried there. It was an experience that I wanted to explore further.

The Killough Monument

To that end, a friend and I decided that it was a good idea to drive out to the Killough Monument in the middle of the night. Being of a very curious nature, I wanted to see how the place would receive us alone and in the moonlight... I wanted to know if it would feel any different than it had on my first visit. We waited until it was close to midnight and, after having loaded up on energy drinks and munchies, headed out into the dark.

After driving for a bit, we began to get a bit giddy in anticipation of what was to come. We talked about the massacre and the Native Americans and how brutal it must have been. We discussed the theory that a sudden death leaves

160

much unrest in the spirit of the deceased. It was our hope to make some sort of contact with whatever we found there. In my earlier experience I'd found it to be one of the oddest, most intense places I had ever experienced and something told me it wouldn't take much to get a response.

Upon arriving, the first thing that hit me was the awful, still feeling in the air. There was no wind. There was no sound. No leaves rustled, no crickets chirped, no birds sang... there was nothing. Being nestled so far off the beaten path, it felt like we had stepped into a primordial forest and come upon an ancient stone idol where natives were soon to dance in some strange ritual. But nobody came to dance. Once the car was turned off and the engine stopped, there was only the monument and us... and the graves, of course.

The night was oppressive; I found it almost hard to breathe. It was like I was drinking the air rather than breathing it in. The mood had definitely changed. As weird as it was during the day, the nighttime had amplified it tenfold. Almost immediately I felt that we were being watched, and my companion agreed. It was uncomfortable and unpleasant but we pressed on.

Approaching the large stone structure, we turned on the digital recorder we had brought with us and began to speak into it.

"Is anyone here with us tonight?" my friend asked. And after waiting a few seconds she continued, "We would like to talk to you. What is your name?"

We didn't hear anything at all. What we didn't know at the time was when we'd play back the recording later, we would heard a man's voice whisper an answer. He replied "yes" to the question about anyone being there, and "go away" to the request for his name.

We recorded more questions for a few minutes, not realizing we had already gotten a response. Although we kept at it for at least twenty minutes, the only other word we got when we played it all back later was "dangerous." If we had heard it at the time, I assure you I would have left immediately – what came next would not have been necessary.

We had become a bit more comfortable with our surroundings by then. I guess you could say we had become accustomed to the weird stillness. I was simply walking around examining things and listening for anything that might attract my attention, but my companion had other ideas. Unfortunately, she was a fan of those ghost hunting shows on TV where the hunters agitate and provoke the spirits to get a response. Without any warning, she began shouting at the top of her lungs into the darkness.

"I know you're out there! It's you, isn't it Mr. Indian Chief? Stop being a chicken and show yourself! You were big and bad when you killed these unarmed white settlers, but now you're cowering in the woods... afraid to show yourself to us!" she yelled.

My blood ran cold. I was stunned that she was brave enough to try this in the first place, but I was also very concerned for our welfare. This felt very wrong. It was the wrong thing to do and the wrong place to do it, and I was frozen in place.

"Big, bad, Indian Chief!" she continued, "Murdered innocent people and ran away! Ran away to hide like you're doing now! Show yourself!"

I looked at my friend on the other side of the monument from me and then glanced back at our car in the parking area, wondering if we could make it back to it in time to save ourselves if something did decide to show itself. That's when I noticed the wind had begun to blow. The silence was broken by the sudden mad rustling of the leaves on the trees. The gust became stronger and I heard something moving in the woods on her side of the stone structure.

"If wind is all you got, I'm not impressed!" she shouted again. "Come out and show yourself, you big chicken chief! That's right, you are the Chief of Chickens!"

My feet started working again and I began making an arc toward her, angling closer to the car, and keeping an eye on the part of the woods where I was hearing the noise. The wind grew stronger and whatever was in the woods was getting closer. I heard twigs snapping and what sounded like small limbs breaking. It was as if something very large was clearing a path straight to us. I knew it was past time to go and I was going to get her out of here with me, even if I had to drag her.

I reached her just as a loud crash hit at the edge of the woods near the clearing where the historic site began. She hadn't noticed I was coming up behind her and when I touched her shoulder she let out a short scream. We looked at each other briefly and we both started running for the car.

163

The wind was strong enough now that leaves were blowing around us as we ran and, though I didn't hear whatever was coming out of the forest anymore, I knew it was near. We reached the car, dove in, started the engine and threw it into drive in what was almost one fluid motion. I gassed the engine before our doors were even closed and hauled butt out of there.

Our hearts didn't stop racing for an eternity after we drove away, but the wind died down as soon as we lost sight of the monument in our rear view. I didn't slow from my break-neck pace until we had put a few miles between us and it. Even though we had gotten safely away, I kept looking in the mirrors, sure I would see something huge following us home.

Now, one would think that I had learned a powerful lesson that night. And I guess I did. I stayed away from the Killough Monument for two years. Somehow, though, I couldn't get it out of my head. I knew I never wanted to go there at night again, but I felt like I needed to go back, at least one more time, just to see how I felt about it.

I began talking about the monument to friends and folks I knew and was surprised to find out how many of them had never even heard of it. Several of the people I spoke to about it, expressed a desire to see it. I considered this for a bit and decided there should be safety in numbers. With that thought in mind, I rounded up ten of my friends and acquaintances who had an interest in the historic value of the place and one Saturday morning, I set out to visit this odd stone tower one more time.

Arriving just before noon, we piled out of my van and I began telling them details of the history as I cautiously worked my way amongst the graves. I kept one eye on the woods as I related all I knew, and one ear open for anything out of the ordinary. It was still again. A couple of my traveling buddies noted the stillness... commenting on how odd it was that the afternoon was so quiet. I smiled and asked if they noticed anything else.

One of them mentioned it was a bit hard to breathe. Another said his ears had closed up like he was under water. A third said she had an uneasy feeling but didn't know why. I told them I had experienced something similar, but didn't go into any detail on how harrowing it had become. I told them it was possible that these spirits were not at peace and I said I wished I had a way to comfort them.

Someone suggested we sing to them. Then another suggested that if we did, we should sing a well known hymn that these people might have known. I happened to know that one of the people there was a beautiful singer with an incredible voice, so I asked her if she would sing *Amazing Grace*. At first she refused, stating it was too hard to catch her breath, but after a little cajoling from the rest of the party, she acquiesced and moved to the front center of the monument.

When she let loose with that amazing voice, we were all enthralled. It was stunning. She conveyed both joy and heartache in that old-time hymn that moved us all. And when she stopped, we all noticed the birds, who had been silent before, suddenly erupted into a chorus of chirps and tweets as if they were singing along with her. For just a moment we were transfixed by this phenomenon as we also noticed a light breeze now blew over us. This calm awe was shattered as the singer suddenly screamed and started heading away from the area.

I ran to catch up with her and asked what was wrong.

"We need to go." She said, never slowing her stride. "We need to leave right now."

I motioned for everyone to follow us as we headed back to the van. As we all got inside and we began pulling away, I asked again what had happened.

"Something grabbed my arm." She answered. "I felt fingers on my arm pulling me toward the monument but there was no one near me. I don't want to feel that ever again."

We sat in silence for a minute, letting what she had said settle in, as I drove back to the main road. Finally, we began to question her further, but there really wasn't much else to say. After relating her story one more time, she said she didn't want to talk about it anymore. Someone made mention of the weird way the breeze came up and the birds began to sing out of what was complete still silence before she sang. We all agreed that it was very strange.

Two weeks before this happened, I had been carrying on a texting conversation with the singing lady. She had been at work at the time and I had asked her how business was that day. She had replied and we had continued texting for a while about other things. Strangely enough, at this moment, at about two miles away from the monument and headed home, my phone suddenly started vibrating and beeping as if I had received a text.

When I looked at the phone to see who was texting me, I was floored by what I saw. Before I said anything about it, I asked the singer if she had just texted me. She said she had not, that she didn't even have her phone turned on at that point. I watched her dig it out of her purse to show me. She was correct. It was turned off.

I then showed everyone the text I had just received from her phone. It was the answer to the question I had asked about her business two weeks earlier that I had already received and forgotten about. Somehow it had been sent to me again... completely out of context. The two words that flashed on my screen were: "we died." Was it a final message from the slaughtered settlers? I believe it was.

Once again, I felt much relief to be leaving Killough. Judging from the looks on everyone's faces that day, I think we all did. I just didn't know what to think. On the way home, I related what had happened to me the last time I went out there. They chastised me for not telling them and called me crazy for wanting to go back. One of them asked me, "Well, now that you have had these crazy experiences out there, will you ever go back?"

Without hesitation, I replied, "Of course."

If you visit Killough Monument, please remember that is a memorial to a family who died in a very tragic way. As with any cemetery or sacred ground, be respectful, and please do not take anything out with you but photographs.

I have been back to Killough Monument, and unfortunately I saw that vandals had done quite a bit of damage there. It looked like the work of young revelers, because beer cans were scattered around the parking lot, more pentagrams were spray-painted on the asphalt of the parking lot like I'd seen before, and there was broken glass everywhere. The scene almost brought tears to my eyes. I gathered up the trash that I could before leaving, shaking my head at the disrespect that some people have.

The vandalism has not gone unnoticed – I understand that cameras have been placed around the area, and the law enforcement officers patrol it much more closely. The gates are also locked at night, so Killough Monument is only open to the public during the day.

Hopefully those who are set on disrespecting the site with litter and destruction of the property there will someday tire of their antics and leave the place to what it should be – a monument to a piece of Texas history, and the resting place of those who died there. And perhaps, a few spirits that linger still.

To visit the Killough Monument:
1. From the intersection of Highway 69 & Farm/Market (FM) Road 855 go west on FM 855 until you reach FM 3405. There is a sign there (or was at one time) that reads

"Killough Monument" and points to the left.
2. Turn left on FM 3405 and go just about .4 miles to FM 3411.
3. Turn right on FM 3411 and go .6 miles until you reach a road with a green gate with a huge boulder on either side. That is actually FM 3431, but there is no sign there.
4. Turn left and proceed through the gate – the monument and cemetery are at the end of the road.

Note: I'd ask you to not only be respectful at the monument, but cautious for your own safety as well – it's in the middle of nowhere, and some unsavory people have been known to go there. Personally, I've always been more afraid of the living than I have of the dead!

Chief Bowles Memorial

I've been around the block when it comes to dealing with spirits. I've seen things that would make most men curl up in a fetal position... things that your nightmares are made of. Sometimes I sought them out, and sometimes I happened upon them like it was meant to be. Some of these places were dropped in my path as if I was guided there by unseen hands. The land at Chief Bowles Memorial is one of those places.

The Killough Monument that is the subject of the previous chapter was only the beginning of a horrible set of circumstances that resulted in the wholesale slaughter of over 800 men, women and children. With the incident at Killough being touted as a rallying cry among the white settlers and years of hatred and prejudice mixing with greed and fear, it was decided that all Native Americans... or Indians, as we like to call them, should be removed from East Texas. Folks were convinced it was these "heathen Indians" that had murdered the Killough family and were responsible for so many other crimes against the whites.

Unfortunately, the Cherokee tribe had chosen the Tyler area to settle in and had taken in many other stragglers from other tribes in their effort to build a new life in this strange world that was no longer the one they had always known. Now, when the Killough massacre happened, the Cherokee claimed no part of it and even renounced the act as that of renegades or some such, but it was not enough. There was too much hatred being thrown on all sides. And even though, the great Chief Bowles had proven time and again that he was a friend to the white man, he was told that he had to leave the area and take all his people with him.

Chief Bowles

The Chief argued of course, but to no avail. He made note that he was good friends with Sam Houston and even showed the ceremonial sword of brotherhood that Sam had presented him with as a show of friendship. No one cared. He pleaded that he had many elders and children and they did not have enough food to make the trip out of Texas. He asked for a three month delay to at least reap the harvest and stock pile provisions for the trip. The request was denied.

He knew that most of them would not survive the ordeal so he dug in and tried to stall while he sent a runner to try to find Sam Houston and bring him back to the Tyler area to talk some sense into the settlers that were determined to remove them from land that had been given to them by treaty. There were several small skirmishes as the Chief and his people were driven back to the edge of what is now Smith & Van Zandt Counties along the Neches River. It was here, along the river banks, that the tribes made their last stand.

The runner missed Sam Houston by one day. One day could have made the difference and saved 800 people, but it was not to be. Sam wasn't reached and on the morning of July 16, 1839, the final battle began. It became known as the "Battle of the Redlands," or the "Battle of the Neches." Even to the last, the Chief tried to stop the fighting, but in final resignation he said: "If I fight, the whites will kill me, if I refuse to fight, my own people will kill me."

And so it happened... five hundred Texas Militia attacked and all the Indians, save the few that managed to escape towards the end, were killed beside the Neches that day. The old Chief himself was shot in the back and fell off his horse. As he raised himself up to his knees he was shot at close range, execution style, in his face and his bones were left to rot there, on display, for years afterward. It has been said that two inch strips of his flesh were removed from his shoulder to his ankle and was made into a belt as a "prize of battle." Some folks even said he was scalped and his scrotum removed.

Many, many years later the atrocity still presented itself as a stain on the flourishing counties that were built on the Indian land and it was decided a monument should be erected. Indeed it was placed, by the State of Texas on the site of the battle, within what they believed to be fifty yards of where the Chief was executed. The remaining bones were buried in a clearing and the site became a historic landmark.

Still, it fell into disrepair and became so unkempt that no one could get to it and soon the memory began to fade. Fortunately, a man named Eagle Douglas made it his calling to preserve it, and with the help of his friends and fellow natives, Sondra "Two Feathers" McAdams, Tim Benson, "Doo-Dad," and others, he has mostly succeeded. It can now be visited easily and they have a memorial ceremony each July on the land. I, myself, have begun working with them to bring in funding and increase awareness of this place because the moment my foot touched the soil, I felt something race through me.

Eagle Douglas

The first time I visited the site, I had heard about Eagle and his crew and reached out to them to find out more about the land. We arranged a meeting time and I took my family with me and met them at the memorial. The stillness and serenity at first was like being in church. It washed over me and I felt immediately at peace. We introduced ourselves and had a smudging ceremony before we marched into the river bottoms and to the stone monument itself.

Sondra led the way and she passed us each a bag of corn meal, explaining that it was an offering of respect to the tribes that had been killed here. She explained that there were twelve other tribes that had blended with the Cherokee, making thirteen in all. The names of those other tribes were Shawnee, Delaware, Kickapoo, Quapaw, Choctaw, Biloxi, Ioni, Alabama, Coushatta, Caddo of the Neches, Tahocullake, Mataquo and possibly other groups. She showed us that there are thirteen stone markers leading the way down the narrow trail through the woods to the memorial. Each stone has the name of a tribe carved into it, and by sprinkling some corn meal on the stone; you show respect and ask permission to be there.

As we walked, the intensity of the land increased. After each stone, the feeling of serenity faded a bit more and it was replaced with a feeling of dread and infinitely deep sadness. A wild rabbit hopped out of the woods and came within two feet of me and sat and watched me. I thought that was strange that it would get so close, so I decided to inch closer to it and see what happened. It allowed me to get almost to where I could reach and touch it before it hopped into the shrubs. It never ran, and even when it took cover it stayed where it could see me. Sondra explained that the spirits were checking me out and I was of particular interest. She said it could be a sign; it could represent my spirit guide, and she would jokingly but not jokingly call me "the Rabbit" from then on.

By the time we had passed the ninth stone, I felt like we were no longer alone. I heard footsteps walking beside me. My family heard them, too. We searched the woods with our eyes but saw nothing.

By the time we passed the twelfth stone I was seeing fleeting shadows on either side of us. My wife swore she saw an Indian brave dart behind a tree. Sondra became aware of what we were experiencing and she told us not to worry. She explained that they just wanted to know who was on their land and what we were up to. She spoke out loud to thin air and told whoever or whatever might be listening that we were good people and we were there to help.

We made it to a large grassy clearing with stone benches around the edges and a large stone monument in the shape of a huge tombstone in the center. This was the actual memorial. As I walked to the stone, I heard the tinkling of wind chimes and I noticed there were all sorts of things tied in the nearby trees and there was a pile of objects at the base of the monument itself. I was told that these were offerings of respect, sympathy, and brotherhood. I immediately let the last of my corn meal sift from my hand onto the marker and asked to be accepted as a helper and keeper of the land.

As the grains of meal dropped from my hand and as I watched some being carried on the wind out into the clearing, I surveyed the objects others had left. There were dream catchers, chimes, ribbons, bones, knives, tobacco, dried fruits, coins, colored stones, and a multitude of other odd objects. Sondra explained that not everyone came here expecting to leave something but some feel compelled to do so anyway. She said that even though some of the objects had nothing to do with Indian culture, it was the show of respect that mattered. I reached in my pocket and pulled forth my change and dropped it in front of the marker. It felt like the thing to do.

The feeling was heavy. It was as if the weight of the death of a beloved family member had settled on my chest. And yet, I wanted to sing or dance or something. I wanted to celebrate life in the midst of this memorial to death. It was horrible to know that 800 people including mostly elderly, women, and children had been slaughtered here, but somehow I felt that they had seen enough sadness and would welcome something to distract them. In this spirit, I later arranged a wonderful Native American Flute maker to come and play on the land and it became one of the most amazing moments of my life...but that's another story.

From that moment on, I was hooked. I have given as much time as I could to helping bring the existence of the land to the consciousness of the people of East Texas and beyond. And I spend as much of my personal time there as I can even when I don't have a reason to. I take tours out there and I bring all my friends there eventually. It was during one of these trips that another thing happened that has burned itself into my memory as well.

A friend had come to town and we were catching up and comparing notes as friends who don't see each other all the time often do and I told him I had been helping with the land. He immediately wanted to go... even though it was well after dark and past midnight. I had been there in the evening before but never this late and I wasn't sure I wanted to take him there until morning. He persisted and I finally agreed.

Everything was fine on the ride there and all the way up to the little building that is used as a classroom and marks the beginning of the decent into the river bottoms and the trail to the monument. It was at this point that he began to feel uneasy, making comments on how dark it was and how heavy it felt. He is a great friend and he has psychic abilities that I have been in awe of for many years. So you can imagine the chills that began running up and down my spine when he started making these comments.

He went on to tell me that we definitely were not alone. He said we were being watched ever since we turned off the main road. He expressed the intense feeling of sadness I had experienced myself. He told me the land held the atrocities committed here like ink on paper. For a moment, I thought he was going to ask to leave, but he didn't. We left the van in the parking area and walked into the woods with our flashlights and a bag of tobacco I had brought to offer to the spirits of the stones.

We had passed the third stone when my friend stopped dead in his tracks. He was staring at a tree that we were about to pass. I looked in the same direction and for just a second I thought I saw a man standing there in the darkness. My heart skipped a beat and I shined my light on the tree. There was nothing there that I could see.

But there *was* something there that could not be seen. And my friend was communicating with it. He explained to me that he could see an Indian warrior. He said he thought he might be a lesser chief to Bowles and that he was a guardian of the land. The spirit was threatening us. Warning us that if we had bad intentions that we needed to leave or we would suffer the "consequences." I was told that he looked angry and very fierce and my friend believed that it was possible that the warrior could really hurt us if he chose to do so.

We both spoke out loud, affirming we were friends and we meant no harm. After a few moments, my friend said the warrior warily stepped aside but said he would be watching us. We continued down the path and we both saw and heard many things on the way to the monument. There were many spirits with us that night. Some were threatening harm if we caused mischief and did not show respect for sacred land, some were just curious, and some seemed to be calling for peace. Some voices came to us in English, and some in tribal tongues we could not understand. Every hair on my body was so straight the follicles began to ache. My heart raced and threatened to leap from my chest.

The trail to the monument

When we reached the monument, I brought out my recorder and we began to talk. We thanked them for allowing us to be there. We apologized for what had happened there. We placed the last of the tobacco there and showed respect. We asked if there was anything we could do to help them. My friend offered to relay any messages he could. He told me they recognized me and they knew I was trying to help. He said they called me "funny fat man" in an affectionate way. I wasn't sure if I should be offended or not, but I accepted it…as it is a pretty accurate description.

We had ventured out into the center of the clearing and my companion told me they were zipping in and out for closer looks. He said we were absolutely surrounded. I heard footsteps. I saw shadows racing here and there. I felt cold first on one side and then another. I believed him.

Then, from the far side of the clearing something crashed like a tree falling and we heard a low groan and a deep growl. I

178

shined my light and tried to choke my heart back down but there was nothing there. We heard heavy thumps, like a big man walking toward us from the same direction, but again there was nothing there. My friend turned to me and said: "I think that's the cue to leave. We have been allowed to stay as long as they wanted us to." He didn't have to tell me twice.

We turned and began the long walk back up out of the woods toward the van. Every fiber in my being screamed at me to run, to drop the light and run like the devil was nipping at my heels, but I refused. I breathed deep and kept a steady pace. I wanted to show that I respected the spirits of the land, but I also wanted them to know I was not a coward. I hoped that my bravery would elicit some respect in kind and not just be considered foolhardy.

When we reached the gate, my buddy turned to me and said: "It's good that you didn't run. I know you wanted to. I did too. But we did the right thing. As we passed the guardian warrior on the way out, he smiled and nodded at us. He knows."

As we drove away, the spirits continued to talk to us. They spoke of Eagle and Two Feathers. My friend did not know who they were but he relayed the messages to me. He said the spirits were telling him these were good people and we should work with them. He told me they believed I had good intentions and that they thought I could help. He also told me they knew I was part Cherokee...which is true...my great grandmother was full blood...but there has been a lot of cream in the coffee since then. They spoke of life in the past and how the battle played out. It went on for some time, but as we crossed over the Neches, heading back into Tyler, the voices faded.

Later, as I reviewed my recording of that night, I heard two voices on the recording that were not ours. The first voice said: "You are Cherokee." The second voice said: "I am Ioni." Both voices spoke quickly and with what could be considered

179

Native American accents. I have no explanation for these EVPs.

I have great respect for this land, and I urge you to have the same respect. It is by far the most spiritual and spirit laden place I have ever encountered, but it is not a joke. By all means, go visit. Help if you can. Spread the word. But don't go there to play. It is definitely nobody's playground.

To get there from Dallas (85 mi.) go east on I-20 toward Canton. Exit off I-20 onto Hwy 64 turn right at the stop sign. Proceed on Hwy 64 through Canton, Ben Wheeler and Midway to Redland (no town just a sign) this is about 25 miles. Watch for a large sign on the right depicting a historical marker. Turn north (left) onto Van Zandt CR 4923 (2.4 mi) to the LAND. Be alert and watch for the signs because they are small and handmade and can be missed easily.

From Tyler the LAND is about 12 miles west on Hwy 64 toward Canton. You will cross the Neches and soon see a sign saying "Redland." Then you will see a Historical Marker sign with a pointing arrow. Turn north (right) onto Van Zandt CR 4923 (2.4 mi) to the site.

The Moving Statue
of Jacksonville Cemetery

Jacksonville City Cemetery, Jacksonville

Whenever someone starts recounting the ghost stories of an area, there is almost always a haunted cemetery included in the mix – you'll find a few in this book, in fact. Some cemeteries have very interesting stories, and are well worth exploring. Others are known for more sensational tales that seem completely unbelievable – like accounts of granite statues above the gravestones that actually move.

These stories are quite common, and almost always the statue moves at some specific time, usually midnight, and some type of harmless ritual must be performed to make the miracle occur. The process involves flashing the automobile headlights, honking the horn, running around the car a few times, or other

181

such shenanigans. Any sort of nonsensical hoopla like that is usually a sure sign of an urban legend.

One thing that I've noticed in my years of ghost hunting is that spirits never, ever show up on schedules that we dictate and any legend that has horn honking and light flashing in it is almost certainly not true. I've visited some of the most haunted places in the country and come away empty-handed, but had some dramatic supernatural events occur on the spur of the moment when I was least expecting it. It has become very clear to me that the world of the supernatural is not on our schedule, and we're not on its schedule. In most circumstances it's truly a right-place-at-the-right-time thing.

So while I'm understandably apprehensive when I hear stories about moving graveyard statues, I happened to be driving through Jacksonville and remembered a tale that I'd heard about the City Cemetery there. I'd written about it in a book several years ago, in fact. It didn't take long to locate the cemetery once again, and with only a little bit of scouting around, I ran across the famous, moving statue itself: a stately stone portrayal of Mother Templeton.

It looked exactly like it had on my visit years before – the lady's right hand was just below her heart, and her left hand was hanging at her side. Looking at that, I once again remembered the story as it had been told to me: if you visit the cemetery at the right time (it varies with the person telling the tale), you will see that she has somehow, mysteriously moved – her hands would no longer be empty; instead the good Mother in the moonlight could be seen standing on her pedestal clutching a bouquet of flowers, or holding an open Bible as she keeps a nocturnal watch over the Templeton family plot.

It was mid-afternoon on my latest visit, so I only saw Mother Templeton in her statue's normal stance. It was curious, though – if she did move, where did the additional items come from? Was it a bouquet of marble flowers that she borrowed from another statue, or real blooms that she'd stooped and picked up from a nearby grave? And how about the bible that she is said to hold – is it marble as well, and if not, where in the world does she get it? Perhaps it is borrowed from a nearby grave that had one carved into the headstone. Ah, the wonders of a moving statue story.

There are plenty of moving statue stories around, and are almost always (did I really just say "almost"?) urban legends. In fact, I once wrote about a statue of Christ from the days of my youth. It was in a cemetery, much like Mother Templeton, and the Redeemer had his arms stretched out to the sides as if ready to give a big hug. If you went there at midnight, however, honked your car horn three times, then drove around the cemetery loop, he would move his hands out in front by the time you came back around. It was an optical illusion, albeit a very spooky one, and gave many a teenager a good scare. I'm sure that the illusion also made young girls scoot closer over to their boyfriends, which may be the real reason for the entire exercise.

I found another such statue in Natchez, Mississippi, in their city cemetery. It is beautiful, almost life-sized statue of an angel overlooking five small headstones with different names, but the same date of death.

On March 14, 1908, an explosion at the Natchez Drug Company killed five girls that were working there. It totally destroyed the five-story building and put the company out of business. The owner was so devastated by the tragedy that he paid for the five girls to be buried together, and commissioned a statue of an angel to watch over their graves for all time to come. The way that the artist sculptured the angel, however, had an unanticipated property – cars passing along the cemetery drive would see the angels illuminated in their headlights. As they passed, it would turn on its pedestal.

The stories of the "turning angel" of the Natchez cemetery began to spread, much as the legend of Mother Templeton in the Jacksonville cemetery has.

Looking at the statue of Mother Templeton, I didn't see any traits that might cause a similar illusion, but who knows. It could be dependent on the moonlight, the shadows, the angle of view, and of course, a good dose of fright from being in a cemetery at night.

Thinking back to my days as a teenage boy, I would have latched onto a legend like that and taken every one of my dates there. I'd be the first one screaming, "Look, she's holding a bible!" or "Oh my God, she's moved and is holding flowers!" I'd be perpetuating that myth as much as possible to get the girl to scoot over a little closer in the car seat. And to be honest, that's what I think has fueled this urban legend over the years.

I have to admit, though, even with the certainty that I had about the myth of Mother Templeton's statue, I got a little melancholy standing before it. The same thing happened on my last visit to the cemetery, in fact.

This was much more than a statue with an urban legend

attached – it was erected as a monument to a real, flesh-and-blood woman. I couldn't help wonder who she was in life, and what wonderful things must she have done to warrant having a statue erected to her honor. All of that still remains a mystery. I'd absolutely love to know, though – and to be perfectly honest I think that her real story would be infinitely more interesting than the tale of her moving statue. God bless Mother Templeton.

Jacksonville City Cemetery
Kickapoo Street
Jacksonville, Texas

The Phantom Dorm Director

Lon Morris College, once the oldest existing two-year college in the State of Texas, was founded in 1854. It was originally called the New Danville Masonic Female Academy, then the Alexander Institute, and was finally given the name Lon Morris College in 1924 in honor of R.A. "Lon" Morris of Pittsburg, Texas, who donated his entire estate to the school. At that time, it had been acquired by the Texas Methodist Annual Conference and was the only two-year Methodist college west of the Mississippi River. Lon Morris held membership in the Southern Association of Colleges and Schools longer than any other two-year college in Texas, and was the only surviving pre-Civil War school in East Texas.

Over a hundred and fifty years later, Lon Morris College was still growing. A gift from the city of Jacksonville allowed them to have a municipal activity center, a rodeo arena, and more land in which to grow. The college held annual events such as the Tops-in-Texas Rodeo at the rodeo arena without any outside financial assistance. Students could participate in a variety of sports including men's/women's basketball, baseball and softball, men's/women's soccer, men's/women's golf, volleyball, cheerleading and dance. In 2009, football was added as a varsity sport

Lon Morris alumni include Sandy Duncan, actress of stage and screen; star of television and big screen Margo Martindale; country music star K. T. Oslin; Broadway legend Tommy Tune; NBA player Dexter Cambridge; Chicago Cubs first baseman Micah Hoffpauir; legendary country music superstar Johnny Horton; and that is to name but a few.

The college has several residence halls: Brown Hall, Clark Hall, Craven-Wilson Hall, Fair Hall, Cooper House, LMC Cottages, and LMC Lodge. Even with these facilities, in 2009 a number of students were housed in two Jacksonville motels.

One of these, Craven-Wilson Hall, is reported to have more than just students wandering its hallways. David Gehrels, coordinator of student activities at Lon Morris, told the *Jacksonville Daily Progress* newspaper that the dorm is rumored to be haunted by a female ghost that used to be a hall director back in the early 1930s. "Her name was Ms. Brown, and she had cancer," he told the paper, "and she died in the hall." The woman reportedly worked right up to the point of her death, but may not have left her duties as director.

Gehrels told the *Daily Progress*, "Students noticed different things – radios, iPods, televisions turning on by themselves, lights coming on and off and strange smells, like cleaning products." Drawers and doors sometimes open by themselves, and books that were shelved in alphabetical order are found to be rearranged and jumbled. He assured that the spirit was not malicious all – simply doing the kinds of things that a dorm director might do in the course of the semester. "Kind of like having your grandma living there," Geherls said.

Craven-Wilson Hall

Only once did a student request to be moved from the hall after two weeks there – she wasn't frightened, but the young lady was experiencing so much activity that she was simply losing sleep.

I could hardly wait to visit the college and see if it would be possible to visit Craven-Wilson Hall, but then I learned something truly sad.

As reported on CNN, on May 23, 2012, all college employees, with the exception of 11 core people, were furloughed indefinitely. This affected over 100 individuals, and happened after the school had already missed three pay periods. The president of the college submitted his resignation notice effective May 24, 2012. The affected individuals were notified via email. Later that month Tyler Junior College sent an outreach team to help Lon Morris students register for summer classes at Tyler Junior College. It also allowed Lon

Morris students to live at the junior college residence halls at discounted rates.

Lon Morris College filed for bankruptcy on July 2, 2012. The 112-acre campus was scheduled to be put up for auction. Fortunately, charitable organizations may have come through and provided funds to pay the employees but it appears that the campus has been pieced out to different buyers.

The most interesting question to me concerns Craven-Wilson Hall... just what will the new owner encounter there, and how will they handle the supernatural situation?

Lon Morris College
600 College Avenue
Jacksonville, Texas 75766

$Spirits\ of\ the\ Howard\ Family$

The Howard-Dickinson House, Henderson, Texas

The historic Howard-Dickinson House is poised stately on a hill overlooking South Main Street in Henderson, Texas. Although it is now a world-class museum, it was once the home of a couple of brick-mason brothers who made it the showplace of Rusk County.

The Howard brothers came to Texas from Richmond, Virginia and brought with them a talent for construction. They designed their home in Italian architectural style, and built it from 1854 to 1855 using handmade brick and their masonry skills. It was the first brick house in Rusk County, in fact. The brothers used a kiln built on the property especially for this project. The house was also the first to use an iron-reinforced structure, and the first to have plaster walls. It also had a basement, which was very unusual for any East Texas home. When it was complete, it was definitely the talk of the town.

For warmth in the winter months, the brothers included chimneys with fireplaces in the first and second stories, and the basement as well.

David Howard and his wife Martha lived in the house with their ten children. Also living in the house was David's brother, who never married.

With their reputations as master craftsmen in place, the Howard brothers went on to do many of the buildings in Henderson, including the Rusk County courthouse.

David's wife Martha Ann had a cousin of some note named Sam Houston, hero of San Jacinto and the first President of the Republic of Texas. Whenever he was passing through the area, Houston would stay as a guest in the Howard home.

Tragedy struck the home, when two of the Howard sons, both young men, were in the basement cleaning their guns. Suddenly a gunshot sounded throughout the house. Apparently one of the guns had accidentally discharged. One of the sons was mortally wounded, and crawled through the house looking for help, before he finally collapsed and died in the home.

The Howards occupied the house until 1905; David had died, followed by his brother, so Martha Ann sold the house to Mrs. Katherine Dickinson, a single mother with two children, Katherine and Brad. She decided to add on to the original house by adding a rear wing, and opened a boarding house there for income.

When Mrs. Dickenson died, she left the house to her daughter Katherine. According to the legal documents related to the house, Katherine could live in the house unless she were to marry, in which case the house would then pass to her brother.

Katherine never married, but in 1950, she left the home, and in fact, the city. No one knows where she went or whatever happened to her. The house sat empty for the next fourteen years. As any abandoned building will do, it began to deteriorate during that period. This was aided by an unsavory element, people who broke into the house and did even more harm. It seemed like the wonderful old place was doomed, and in fact, it was condemned. The stately old home with such a wonderful history was going to be torn down by the city.

In 1964, however, Mr. and Mrs. Homer Bryce came to the rescue. They purchased the house and property, and then donated it to the Rusk County Heritage Association. It took the organization three full years to restore the home to its original beauty, but when they finished, it had every bit the elegance of its bygone days. The Association furnished the house with period antiques, including a trunk that belonged to Sam

Houston, and an organ that was the first one of its kind in Rusk County.

The Howard-Dickinson House was awarded a Texas Historical Medallion by the Texas Historical Commission in 1968, and it was recorded as a Texas Historic Landmark.

There are many displays for visitors to enjoy: historical books, significant papers, paintings, manuscript collections, antique clothing, linens and lace, unique dolls, and beautiful china, glass, and silver. There is a two hundred forty-volume library of medical books, a wealth of genealogy material, and many other references that can be viewed on premises.

Of course, you know by now that I wouldn't be going into this much detail about the house if it didn't have a ghost story associated with it... and it does. Workers and guests there have reported a woman who walks into the house and climbs the stairs. Joan Hallmark, a reporter for KLTV 7 News in Tyler, Texas, tells that the late Mata Jaggers described the incident as follows:

"Mrs. Howard is the spirit most often sensed in the house, perhaps because of the late Mata Jaggers who saw a woman in white enter the house and then disappear as she climbed the stairs.

"Jaggers was convinced she was seeing Mrs. Howard and descriptions by relatives seem to confirm the sighting. When forks are carried on plates out of the Howard-Dickinson dining room, they often jump to the floor. It's thought that Mrs. Howard's spirit is a stickler for proper dining etiquette. Lights that come on in an upstairs bedroom when no-one is in the house have been seen by a number of people.

"A bloodstain on a bedroom floor, coming from a shooting between the Howard brothers, cannot be removed – though many have tried."

There are other harmless manifestations that remind the staff there that they might not be alone. Lights turn on and off by themselves, objects are lost and then found again in the strangest places, and as with many other places with ghost stories, cold drafts of air seem to appear out of nowhere. A docent recounts turning off all of the lights in the house, locking the door, and going home for the evening. When she arrived the next morning, a light was shining brightly in the basement. Once, a police officer was driving by the house and saw a woman standing on one of the upper floor balconies, waving in an urgent manner for him to come to the house. When he went inside and told the docent what he had seen and proceeded to investigate the upstairs rooms, he found nothing there.

While I didn't experience the spirit of Mrs. Howard or any other of her family when I saw the museum, I was definitely impressed with the old place. There are so many things to see there that it's no mystery to me why Mrs. Howard might be coming back for an occasional visit. It's a wonderful old home, and since I didn't even begin to see everything there, I'll be back again... perhaps next time my visit will coincide with Mrs. Howard's!

Howard-Dickinson House Museum
501 S. Main St.
Henderson, TX 75654
903-657-6925

A Theater Ghost Named Daphne

Henderson Civic Theatre, Henderson, Texas

We've been all over the area surrounding Tyler in the pages of this book, and perhaps the number one question that I get from people is, "How in the world do you find all those haunted places?"

The truth is, they tend to find me. Once people learn that I won't laugh at them when they tell stories of encounters with the supernatural, that I will actually believe them, they feel completely comfortable telling me about their experiences.

A great example came when I was at an East Texas bed and breakfast one weekend, and was in the parlor waiting for the morning meal; the other guests were there as well. I was making casual conversation with the other folks, and when I was asked what I did for a living, I told them that I investigated and wrote about haunted locations.

There was some polite and nervous laughter, as always when the topic comes up, with some of them obviously trying to determine whether or not I was serious. A lady then spoke up and said something like, "So, have you ever heard about… Daphne?"

I asked her what she meant, and she started to explain. We talked about it for a few minutes, and I was making notes on napkins, business cards, and anything else that I could find. So began my research into the Henderson Civic Theatre, and its resident ghost named "Daphne."

Throughout my career in exploring haunted locations, I've come to learn that every respectable theater has a ghost, and the Civic Theatre in Henderson is no different. According to people that I spoke with, she's more of a mischievous lady than a scary apparition. She's become the de facto mascot of the theater, and in fact, their annual theatrical award is called "The

Daphne," and it's given out in categories much like its national cousin "The Oscar."

Theater ghosts fascinate me (as you can probably tell from some of the other chapters in this book) so I was drawn to learn more about this theater and the spirit that seems to be in residence there. In my research, I found that theatrical productions in Rusk County began in 1886. The Henderson Dramatic Club launched the area into the world of culture with a production named *The Social Class* in an opera house that had been constructed for them. They went on to do plays for the next few decades, until the advent of World War I changed the face of the country. Resources were redirected to wartime efforts, and the theater group went their separate ways.

A century later, a group of local citizens with a love of the arts drew together to revive the Henderson Civic Theatre like a phoenix from the ashes. Their first production was in a city park, and from there they moved to a local school facility where the plays continued for two years. Next they rented an old building downtown, and during the renovation process, soon discovered that it was the original 1886 Opera House. Funded by donations by supporters throughout the area, they purchased the building and made it their own. They inherited more than the physical structure, however, and the story is best continued from their website as it appeared in 2004, where they explained:

"When the Henderson Civic Theatre purchased the Opera House, they were unaware they were also getting a ghost. No one knows who the spirit is, but apparently she is female and obviously loves theater. She was named 'Daphne' because she made her presence known on stage when 'Blithe Spirit' was being performed. While no one in the audience saw her, the actors on stage were well aware of her presence as she walked among them during the séance scene in Act I."

"Daphne has become a part of HCT, and anyone who spends much time in the building becomes aware of her in one way or another. She is particularly fond of whispering in the wings and more than one director has scolded the cast and crew for making too much noise backstage, only to find out no one was there at all. She also likes to follow people up the stairway located backstage, and has been known to pace back and forth down the hallways on the upper floor. She isn't limited to any one area and has been seen or felt all over the building. Some think that many years ago there was a doctor's office in the building, and she may have some connection with it."

"While some may not feel comfortable knowing of her attachment to the Opera House, we have become quite fond of her and she is considered an asset to the theater. Every time she has made her presence known, especially during Grand Dress, the play has been a rousing success. So, on that night in particular, the cast and crew watch for her to make herself known."

The *Tyler Morning Telegraph* gave an interesting account of the spirit from Mrs. Lynda Trent, theatre group member and director, from an interview with reporter Kenneth Dean: "Walking up the creaky steps into the dimly lit upstairs area, where stage props are kept, the age of the building shows. Brick walls half-covered in plaster, squeaky floorboards and the ambience of a turn-of-the-century warehouse all help to prepare someone as they peer around corners in search of Daphne. Mrs. Trent, who said she has seen the ghost, said Daphne does not perform acts of mischief, but rather does things when they are least expected. 'She (Daphne) has turned on and off one of the spotlights during a show, whispered loudly during rehearsal, followed people up the stairs, been seen on the catwalk. She has basically been seen everywhere in the building, except the lobby. Why that is, I don't have a clue,' she said. Mrs. Trent said the story she believes explains Daphne's presence is the tale of a young woman in the 1930s, who went into premature childbirth and died on the second floor of the building in the doctor's office. 'I don't know if there is an inch of truth to the story, but it seems the best explanation for her presence,' she said. The theatre company gave Daphne her name after a performance of *Blithe Spirit* in which a character was named Daphne. 'Daphne's haunting is more of a teasing. Nothing is ever really malicious. She loves to move things the actors put down and then put them back in the same spot, but never anything really mean,' Loyce Radford said."

The Henderson Civic Theatre has enjoyed many successful seasons, and continues to thrill theater-goers with every performance. When you attend a show there, however, keep one eye open for Daphne – if she is pleased with the production, you just might see her lurking there in the shadows of the stage.

Henderson Civic Theatre
122 E. Main
Henderson, TX 75652
903-657-2968
www.hendersoncivictheatre.com

The Athens Catacombs

Athens, Texas

As I was researching another book, I had someone tell me, "Hey, you need to check out a place named Fuller Park in Athens." I investigated the lead, and before too long, I was up to my word processor in a city recreational area, a potential zoo, a small graveyard, something called the "monkey cage," mysterious underground passageways, all at a place called "Fuller Park."

Going to Athens, it wasn't hard to find the park and a little bit about its background. It is overgrown, and the once-majestic fence around it is starting to crumble. The place was named for a local Baptist minister, the Reverend Melton Lee Fuller. You'll find his and his wife's graves in a family

203

cemetery there, and not far away, is a small pavilion-looking structure that people call the "monkey cage."

Now at this point, I could go into stories that I uncovered about strange lights in the park at night, noises emanating from the graveyard and the monkey cage, but in reality I think that these are all products of local legend that have been handed down through the years. They are grand tales, to be sure, and certainly ones that would chill the air around a campfire on a summer evening. While all this was fine, there was something that intrigued me even more – a story about a network about catacombs underneath the city of Athens. I decided to delve a little deeper into the subject.

Now, I can't say that what I found was any more than the same type of local legend that I'd run across in the park itself. It was certainly interesting enough to hold my attention for a while, so I wanted to include it to give you a chance to enjoy as well.

If you go looking for stories about the underground passageways, you'll likely not find a person who can tell you their origin – or at least, the origin of their legend. I went back through my files on haunted places that I've kept for decades, without a single trace. Turning to online resources, the only clue that I got was from *UFO Magazine*, Vol.7, No.6, 1992, which indicated that there was some joint venture between the United States Government and some alien race to build a network of tunnels under the surface of the earth to allow them to move more freely, without being detected by the general population above. It went on to say that one of the entry points to this network of tunnels was at Athens, Texas. I wonder if the local city council knows that? Oh well, I was about to give up completely when I got a little help from a friend of mine, Olyve Hallmark Abbott. Olyve is a fellow writer of ghost books, and quite a thorough paranormal researcher. I've known her for some time, spoken on the same program with her at several paranormal conferences, and had the pleasure of reading most everything of hers that I've found. In her outstanding work on cemetery haunts *Ghosts of the Graveyard*, Olyve gave me a clue about the tunnels penned by an Athens resident.

As it turns out, the *Athens Review* published an article in 1989 by Brian Spurling who mentioned that an entire network of tunnels was said to be located beneath the city. In his research, he found a resident of the city who said that she remembered tales of the tunnels as part of an escape network for slaves who were making their way up north to freedom in the 1800s. The lady recalled her aunt telling her about venturing out to one of the catacomb's openings one day with a group of family and friends. They found the entry door level with the ground, and as they pried it open, she was too scared to enter and waited on the surface for the rest of the group to emerge. When they did, her friends described the tunnels as being very much like those in coalmines, dug out through the dirt with huge, bracing timbers to hold them up. Some were terrified, because they had found strange, illegible markings on the walls, and bones scattered about the floor.

In researching the tunnels even further, I found that some say that they are laid out in a pentagram form, with the center at the courthouse. Entrances are at the five points of the star, and at the center, in the basement of the courthouse – at least, according to legend.

So, what are these mysterious catacombs that are said to wind about beneath the surface of Athens? Perhaps they're a sterile network of concrete and steel, with security checkpoints and military patrols, and a few closed doors that no one is allowed behind.

On the other hand, maybe some old mining shafts were appropriated for helping enslaved men and women get a few miles closer to their freedom, away from the watchful eyes of those who would do them harm.

Artist's rendition of the catacombs

Another theory is that they were used by bootleggers to move moonshine for distribution throughout the city during the days of Prohibition.

Others have stories and legends of Satanic rituals that take place in the darkness of the tunnels, often culminating inside the walls of Fuller Park.

Or could the tunnels be ancient catacombs, here long before the City of Athens was ever established? Since the stories of the tunnels are nothing more than legend, there's no way to know for certain. Maybe my friend Olyve Abbot has it more accurate – her research indicates that the tunnels would have to pass through very sandy soil with a high water table, something that makes their existence very unlikely. But assuming that it's even possible that they might have existed at one time, it's fun to hypothesize about them, and what their use might have once been.

206

As I've pointed out before, while I was walking down one of Athens' streets near Fuller Park, I could have sworn that I felt a rumbling under my feet. I couldn't help but laugh and think of a Government truck driving below me, carrying a load of gray-skinned, almond-eyed tourists from another galaxy. Looking around, I saw a farm truck rumbling by on a nearby highway. I laughed again at my own imagination, and headed out for a leisurely stroll around the quaint little city. I'll be keeping my eye on the city of Athens, and listening closely to the whispers about the secret catacombs beneath the city. Given half a chance, you'll find me walking through them, exploring, and gathering information for my next book. Would that be fun, or what?

From the Courthouse in Athens, take Highway 19 South to Gibson Road. You will turn left onto Gibson road and go down about 1/4 to 1/2 mile. Fuller Family Cemetery is located within Fuller Park. The graves of the two people buried there are enclosed with an iron gate with a large iron fence around them.

The Ghostly Girl of
Cruce Stark Hall

Kilgore, Texas

As I discover and investigate more and more haunted locations, I've started noticing a few trends, some that I've already mentioned. For example, every theater seems to have a ghost... and so do most institutions of higher learning. That's right – most college campuses seem to have a ghost story or two as part of their lore. Kilgore College is no exception, with a haunting tale of a young student who apparently continues to inhabit one of the dorms there.

When I was first checking out some of Kilgore's ghost stories for another book, I did a little digging into the background of the city itself.

The City of Kilgore was founded in 1872 when the International & Great Northern Railroad established a rail line between Palestine and Longview. Even though the area had been settled by farmers long before the Civil War began, the railroad company formalized the town and named it for the man who'd sold the land: Constantine Buckley Kilgore. There is some speculation that the founding of a new town that would bear his name was part of the real estate negotiations, but there's no concrete evidence of that fact. It makes some sense, though – I could see Mr. Kilgore setting the price with the railroad company, then calling them back to the negotiating table, with a smile and the words, "Oh, there's one more thing that I'd like..."

No matter how it came to be, the town began to grow with the support of the railroad. A Post Office was opened there in 1873, followed by several businesses and a school to serve the children of the families there. Soon there were a couple of churches, a town newspaper, a hotel, a drugstore, two gristmill/cotton gins, and several stores – including an ice cream parlor. The farmers in the area focused on cotton crops, since their harvests could be ginned in town, and then shipped out on the railway. By early 1930 the Great Depression took its toll, however, and the down-spirial of the cotton market dealt a harsh blow to the town and its people.

Kilgore seemed destined to dwindle away to a ghost town, until something happened that pumped a wave of much-needed life into the city: oil was discovered in East Texas in the fall of 1930. Thousands of people descended into Kilgore, looking for oil-field jobs and new starts for their families. Much of the town became a "tent city" for the workers, and over the next five years the population grew from 500 people to over 12,000. Oil wells sprouted up all over town, and one particular downtown block dubbed the "World's Richest Acre" had the most dense concentration of derricks in the entire world.

The oil boom finally waned, but its duration had provided Kilgore with the time and money that it needed to become an established East Texas city.

In 1935 when the petroleum business was in full swing, residents of the city decided that it would be advantageous for a local college to be established. Kilgore College was founded under the supervision of the Kilgore Independent School District, and it operated under their guidance for the next decade. It became known statewide as a two-year school with programs in business, science, and the arts. In 1940, the Kilgore Rangerettes were organized; they are a nationally known precision drill corps of sixty-five girls who have entertained millions and can be seen in many national events, including the annual Macy's Thanksgiving Day Parade.

The College is a fascinating place to visit; along with all of the academic facilities on campus, Kilgore College is also home to the East Texas Oil Museum and the Kilgore College Rangerette Showcase & Museum. On-campus living is a feature that is provided to the students, even though most community colleges aren't residential facilities – something else that makes Kilgore College special. One of these is Cruce Stark Hall, a typical corridor-style dorm, but there's something very a little different about the place: Stark Hall reportedly has a spirited resident that refuses to leave.

The supernatural activity at the dorm seems to center around a female resident that allegedly committed suicide there back when the dorm was an all-girl facility. She has never chosen to show herself to the residents through the years, so the fact that the spirit is considered to be feminine goes back to the legend of the Hall. Reports of her activity there continue semester after semester.

One of the most authoritative reports comes from the Magazine of Kilgore College, *The Flare*. Its October 25, 2002 issue recounts the legend of Stark Hall: "Many students who reside in Stark Hall believe that the ghost of a deceased student haunts the eighth floor of the hall. There is no single story as to who she is or how she died. Several students claimed that she committed suicide by jumping from the eighth floor window. Others say she hanged herself in her closet; still others believe she shot herself in her room. While the story surrounding the spirit is vague, students say her activity is very apparent. One student said he hears noises in the elevator throughout the night. Another said his belongings go missing on a regular basis. While no one said they have seen her, many believe she exists."

Students have reported walking into sudden pockets of icy air in the dorm, when the temperature is warm throughout the rest of the building. Others have heard footsteps, only to look out into the hallway to see that it is empty. Another of the spectral girl's habits is to tap on the hallway wall as she strolls along in the quiet, early hours of the morning.

Could she have been jilted by a boyfriend and decided to take her own life? Or perhaps she was failing her classes and couldn't bear to tell her family. It's even possible that she was with child and felt that taking her own life was the only way out of the humiliation. Who knows – maybe the spirit is really someone else, and not even that of a girl from the college's past. No matter who the ghost is that inhabits Stark Hall, reports of unexplainable noises, cold spots, and rapping on the walls along the hallway continue to be a part of the legends of Kilgore College.

Apparently the ghostly story of Kilgore College carries a little weight, though. In 2013 the *Longview News-Journal* named Cruce Stark Hall as one of the "Top 10 Haunted Locations in East Texas."

The Mysterious Glowing Grave

Danville Cemetery, Kilgore, Texas

If you ask people in Kilgore for a ghost story, more than one will mention the glowing grave in one of the local cemeteries. I had investigated this story several years ago, so I was already familiar with it. There are a few places in this book that I've written about before, but I welcomed the opportunity to re-visit them. In this case, there really wasn't a lot of reason to do so... but I thought that I'd include it just to explain exactly where the mystery of the "glowing grave" came from.

Basically, the "ghost story" goes like this: a young woman from East Texas spent her life working in an Oklahoma nuclear power plant, but because of the poor safeguards at the plant, she was bombarded by radioactive rays every single workday. When she eventually died, her body was returned home and buried in Danville Cemetery in Kilgore. The people of the town began to notice something very strange after her interment – a ghostly, green glow could be seen at night emanating from her burial plot. Some people believed that it was the aftereffects of a career of radioactive exposure, while others who witnessed the phenomena were certain that it was her spirit still showing its presence as a spectral warning to those who worked around such hazardous material.

When I heard the story, I'm sorry, but I couldn't take it seriously. First of all, if by some chance her body was glowing with radiation – which is not really a possibility – then it would certainly be shielded by the coffin and the concrete vault, not to mention several feet of East Texas dirt. On the other hand, if it was some type of apparition that just lay there and glowed, it would be the first that I've ever heard of that presented itself in such a manner. I just didn't buy the story. For the sake of journalism, though, I set off to find the truth behind the tale of the ghostly, glowing grave.

I'll be honest – this story could very well hold the record for the quickest investigation that I've ever conducted. Information about the radiation-lady and her burial in Kilgore was abundant, so I'll just summarize it here before moving to more actual ghost stories.

The lady who is the basis for the story was actually born on February 19, 1946 in Longview, Texas. After graduating High School, she went on to study medical technology at Lamar State College in Beaumont, although she dropped out of the program after the first year. She married, had three children, and in 1972 discovered that her husband was having an extramarital affair. It was more than she could deal with, and she simply walked away from the family on a Saturday morning when her kids were watching cartoons. Her oldest daughter would later tell *People Magazine* in a 1999 interview that, "I was five, Michael was three and Dawn was 18 months. She said she was going out for cigarettes and would I watch my brother and sister. 'Keep an eye on your brother and sister.' That's all she said."

The woman headed north to Oklahoma, where she found employment as a metallography laboratory technician at the Cimarron River Plutonium Plant of Kerr-McGee Nuclear Corporation, located in the city of Crescent.

In the course of her job she joined the Oil, Chemical and Atomic Workers Union, and even participated in the union's strike against Kerr-McGee. The union lost the strike – and most of its members – but the woman had made an impression on her co-workers. In 1974 she became the first female member of the Union Bargaining Committee in Kerr-McGee history.

She found herself a member of a very powerful union committee, and the company re-assigned her from the original responsibilities of grinding and polishing plutonium pellets for use in fuel rods to a position to study health and safety issues at the nuclear power plant. In carrying out her daily duties, she discovered evidence of spills, radiation leaks, and missing plutonium. When her employer was summoned before the Atomic Energy Commission, the woman testified that she herself had suffered radiation exposure over the course of employment at the plant.

During her testimony, she went on to say that the quality control on the fuel rods used in the reactor was faulty at best, and that reports of inspections had been falsified to allow all rods to be used, no matter what their physical state was. Critics of the company have reported that were it not for a bit of blind luck, the United States could have had its own Chernobyl or Fukushima.

The news story went national, and she was contacted by a reporter from the New York Times who wanted to do a story on the Kerr-McGee plant and its irresponsibly in the manufacture of radioactive plutonium rods. The reporter got the woman to agree to a meeting where she would produce some of the evidence that she'd gathered, and turn the documents over to him. Also invited to attend was a member of the Atomic Energy Commission, since they were concerned about her story as well.

She left the Hub Café in Crescent bound for Oklahoma City on November 13, 1974 at about 7:30PM, driving her 1973 white Honda Civic. At 8:05PM, the Oklahoma State Highway Patrol received a report of a single car accident. The State Trooper classified the accident as a driver who'd fallen asleep at the wheel, and the case was closed – at least for the moment.

Several other things point to a conspiracy in the death of the woman, not the least of which are suspicious dents on the rear of her car, as if she'd been forced off the road. Also, the documents that she was bringing to the reporter were never found. They should have been there in the car with her body and personal effects. Many suspected that she had been intentionally forced off the road and wrecked, and the incriminating documents removed from the car. She was twenty-eight years old at the time of her death.

Wreckage of the death car after mysterious crash in 1974

"Anyone exposed to that amount is married to lung cancer."

Silkwood had carried small amounts of plutonium out of the plant and had deliberately contaminated herself and her apartment. Why should she act so bizarre- nesses are expected to tell, for example, of the night that workers were dispatched by the

Clipping from the newspaper story

Her body was returned to Texas, and was buried in the Danville Cemetery in Kilgore. The headstone on her grave simply reads:

Karen Gay Silkwood
Feb. 19, 1946
Nov. 13, 1974
Rest in Peace

That name probably sounds familiar, especially if you remember the movie *Silkwood* from 1983, where Meryl Streep portrayed her character, and Cher played her best friend.

On a previous excursion to Kilgore, I went out to Danville Cemetery as dusk fell one early spring evening, and paused at

219

the grave of Karen Silkwood. The cemetery plot wasn't glowing green, and I found no indication that her restless spirit might be roaming the graveyard. Instead, I found a little solace in the fact that even though the mysterious circumstances surrounding her death will probably never be solved, Karen seems to be resting peacefully underneath the East Texas sky.

The *Silkwood* movie poster starring Meryl Streep, Kurt Russell, and Cher

Danville Cemetery is located
on FM 2087, south of highway 349

A Light in the Cemetery

Pirtle Cemetery, Kilgore, Texas

A lot of folks don't realize that one of the best places to start a ghost hunt is in a public library. Not that libraries are haunted – although many are, sort of like theaters – but they are a very good source of information.

When I'm looking for area haunts, I'll often stop by a local library and start searching through back issues of newspapers... especially around the month of October, when papers write about local hauntings and ghosts.

I was interested to see an article in the *Longview News-Journal* about regional haints, and one of the places was another graveyard in Kilgore – the Pirtle Cemetery.

As the story goes, visitors to the cemetery in the evening have reported seeing a glowing light, dancing and flickering like a small flame.

223

I've been to Pirtle twice now, and on neither occasion did I see the phantom light. The legend about it, however, goes back for generations, to the old days of log cabins and oil lamps.

As the story goes, a couple lived in the Pirtle community with their small son. Although he was a normal child in every way, the boy had the same phobia that many children do – a fear of the dark. When his parents put him to bed every night, he would cry and cry until his mother would light a lantern and put it in his room until he fell asleep. She would often sit beside his bed, singing to him and comforting his fear.

Tragically, the boy fell ill, and since doctors were few and far between in those days, he became worse and worse. The unthinkable then happened... the son died, and the parents were inconsolable – especially his mother.

After the funeral, the woman couldn't stand the fact that her little boy was buried out in the cemetery where it was so dark every evening. On the evenings when she couldn't stand the pain of losing her son, she would take a lantern out to the graveyard and put it on the tombstone.

Eventually the parents died, and were buried beside their boy. According to the legend, people who were passing by the cemetery in the evening would occasionally see a light shining out among the headstones. The locals assumed that the spirit of the mother was still providing a light for her little boy, so that he wouldn't be afraid in the dark.

Now, I'm the first one to say that this story has all the trappings of an urban legend. There is no specific name mentioned, so it is impossible to find the exact marker in the cemetery, although I keep hearing that it is somewhere in the center. And after researching this story and visiting Pirtle for a couple of different books now, I haven't been successful in locating anyone who has actually seen the light for themselves.

There are a number of videos that have been posted on YouTube by different people and groups who have collected EVPs and other interesting phenomena in Pirtle Cemetery, so I can't categorically dismiss the fact that there might be a bit of strange activity taking place there.

As to the mother's light, well, I hate to dismiss ghost lights so quickly. There are many places around the state where they have not only been documented, but also filmed and studied. Examples would be the Ghost Road Light in Saratoga, Texas, and the Marfa Lights, to name a couple. There is some argument as to whether such lights are swamp gas, reflections of other light sources, and so forth, but the fact of such lights remain.

Now, for the loving mother who is reported to be providing a light for her afraid-of-the-dark son, who knows. I'd be tempted to go back to the cemetery at dusk a few more times, just to see for myself. True or not, it's a delightful story of a mother's love.

The Mystery of the Burned-Out Schoolhouse

Shiloh School, Longview, Texas

This Internet Age that we live in is truly an amazing thing. Occasionally I have to stop and marvel at how truly incredible it is – I sometimes feel like we're actually living in some kind of futuristic science fiction world.

Case in point: not long ago I was watching the rerun of a sitcom on television, and a guest star on the show looked familiar to me. I knew that I'd seen him somewhere before, but for the life of me couldn't remember just where. I opened my laptop, did a search for the show I was watching, found the listing for the particular episode, and then brought up the cast list. Once I had the name of the guest star that I'd recognized, I did a search for his name and found that he had a recurring role

227

on another sitcom that I watched faithfully almost twenty years ago. That simply amazed me – something curious (and a little obscure) happened to catch my eye, and I had the answer to it in under a minute. The Internet is truly amazing.

That said, the 'net can also be a little deceiving, especially when it comes to ghost hunting. You really have to be careful about the information that you find; every fact has to be checked, and any claim vetted. That became painfully obvious when I was researching this book. In doing some fact-checking for a reportedly-haunted location near Tyler, I ran across several sites that talked about a burned-out schoolhouse that supposedly had supernatural activity there.

The place was called the "Shiloh School," and the ghost stories are probably best condensed on its Wikipedia entry:

Local legend tells of the Shiloh School being burned down by angered members of the Ku Klux Klan, killing several

228

children that were trapped inside. At night you can hear voices and cries, and the air gets cold. It is also said that there is a broken down bus in the basement of the school in which the door opens and closes when people are near. The area is often patrolled around Halloween and Friday the 13th due to local teenagers and paranormal seekers who try to find ways into the school and cemetery.

Of course this intrigued me, so I set out to find the mysterious Shiloh School. It is northwest of the loop on FM 1845, on (appropriately enough) Shiloh Road.

As you arrive, there is no doubt that you are looking at the remains of a school – outer walls only, with the inner rooms now converted to grass lawn. It's clear that the place is well-cared for, mowed and trimmed, so someone is looking after the Shiloh School.

Reading the online stories about the atrocities committed there – Klan members setting fire with children trapped inside, etc. – gives the location an ominous feeling. I paced the exterior walls, and wandered inside here and there when a break in the brickwork allowed.

Perhaps the most interesting part of my visit came when I walked around to look at the historical marker. It told a much different story.

If you read the historical marker, you'll find that it says: "Shiloh School – The newly freed African Americans of the Shiloh community established a school for their children shortly after the Civil War. The one-room building was demolished in the late 1800s and classes were held at the Shiloh Baptist Church, with financial assistance from the Julius Rosenwald Fund. A new two-room school was erected in 1920. It was replaced by a large brick building in the 1930s. The high school was closed in 1949; the end of segregation closed the rest of the Shiloh School in 1966. Shiloh graduates became contributing citizens in Texas and the nation. Long vacant, the school building was later used to store chemicals for a plastics company and burned in 1993."

The stories of Klansmen and the killed children is therefore simply an urban legend, perpetuated on the Internet. In truth, when the building was finally demolished, it was merely a storage house.

So while the internet stories are certainly based in fiction, does it mean that there isn't any supernatural activity at the site? Not necessarily. Although I didn't encounter anything out of the ordinary during my visit, it could be that all of the emotion that was left there when the building was a school could still be present.

From Longview Loop 281 take FM 1845 north to Shiloh Rd, go west, and the standing ruins of Shiloh School are on the left.

The Railroad Hotel Spirits

The Beckham Hotel, Mineola

In the heart of downtown Mineola, facing the railroad tracks, is the grand old lady of the city: the stately Beckham Hotel. While there is some differing information on the history of the hotel, one account states that it was built in 1892 by Colonel Beckham as a railroad worker's hotel as tracks were being laid across East Texas. When the railroad was finished, rail travelers found comfort at the hotel, whether relaxing in the lobby or dancing in the ballroom.

Whether Beckham built the hotel, or purchased it in the early 1920s as another account suggests, the place became an East Texas showcase.

After over thirty years of welcoming guests, there was a terrible tragedy and the hotel burned. Like a phoenix from the ashes, however, it rose once again – the Beckham was rebuilt by 1928.

In 2012 the Beckham Hotel was listed on the National Register of Historic Places. The official description of the property from the Register is as follows:

This is a two-part commercial block with four storefront bays (three in main building and one in secondary building) and is primarily three stories in height. It was originally built as the Beckham Hotel in 1928. A full width metal tie-rod canopy spans the first story. The first story storefronts have replacement wood sash windows. The entry doors, of differing types, each have a fixed light transom.

Fixed-light transoms are also located above the canopy for the three primary storefront bays; the secondary storefront bay, on the one-story section, has a covered transom. The windows on the second and third story are one-over-one double-hung wood sash, of differing sizes. The sills are concrete, and decorative concrete bands are used to delineate between the second and third story, as well as the parapet.

On the side elevation several windows have been bricked in, but the extant windows are also one-over-one double-hung wood sash. A secondary building on the east elevation includes a second story addition and has two sets of three-part windows and a hip roof. A door located on the east elevation of the third story leads to this hip roof. The Beckham Hotel was built in 1928 after a fire the previous year burned an early structure. In 1942 the hotel's second floor also housed a dance hall. The hotel operated through the 1960s. Currently, the first story is in use as a restaurant and as retail space. The upper stories are unoccupied.

Mr. Beckham owned and operated the hotel from the 1930s through the 1950s when a couple named Andy and

Flossie Lilly took over the general operation of the hotel for him. Later, Mr. Beckham's stepson, Lester Jay, continued to sublease the hotel until 1985.

Musician John DeFoore purchased the building in 1993 and used it as a private residence for a number of years. He developed a part of the hotel to be used for teaching music, and for concerts and presentations by his students. In 2012, DeFoore told the *Tyler Morning Telegraph*, "I know strange things happen here, and I have experienced quite a few of them, but they are not threatening, so I leave them alone, and they leave me alone."

By the end of 2012, DeFoore agreed to sell the hotel to Ron and Connie Meissner, who began to restore the building to its original purpose – to be a hotel that will serve the travelers who stop in Mineola.

Many people traveling to the hotel will not only be looking for the comforts of such an interesting, historic hotel, but perhaps something more… an encounter with the spirits who are reported to exist there.

One of the three main spirits that have been reported in the hotel is that of a man in a suit, walking the upstairs hallways. Some say that he could be a gentleman who took his own life in the lobby of the hotel in the 1940s, or perhaps another man who committed suicide by ingesting acid in an upstairs room. Still another theory is that he is a gambler that was killed in a poker game taking place in a third floor room in the 1930s. Whoever he may be, visitors hear his footsteps, and look up in time to see him step into a nearby room.

Another spirit is a woman in a long dress, sometimes carrying a lady's parasol. There are many stories about her, and most speculate that she was the daughter of the hotel owner after it was built. She was visiting the hotel, and tripped at the top of the stairs, tumbling all the way down to her death. Today she is seen casually walking up the staircase as she must have done prior to her lethal fall.

Then, there is a young girl, between 9 and 11 years old, who has been spotted in the hotel lobby, peering through the glass doors into the adjacent restaurant. Owner John DeFoore told the *Tyler Morning Telegraph* that one of restaurant employees spotted the little girl; he said, "I know one of ladies that saw the little girl... she opened the door thinking it was a guest, and she looked on the other side of the door and there was no one." DeFoore continued, "She literally closed the restaurant, went to her church and got some holy water. She quit the next day."

But it isn't just the three apparitions that have given the hotel its haunted reputation – things happen that are, well, just downright strange. John DeFoore related another story that was reported by the *Morning Telegraph*: "When he first bought the building, he was in the lobby with a group of people when water started pouring down from the ceiling. 'It hadn't rained in two or three weeks, and there was no water on the second

236

floor,' he said. 'There hadn't been water going to the second floor in 10 or 15 years, and when we went up there, there was no evidence of water.' DeFoore said the plumber came and said there was no physical way water could have been pouring out of the ceiling."

As you can see, the haunting of the Beckham Hotel isn't malicious or frightening. Perhaps, in fact, they are simply shadows of the hotel's wonderful, old history. If you visit the hotel and spend the evening there, perhaps you'll catch a glimpse of one of its resident spirits... or instead, you may simply find yourself in the comfort of a place preserved in time.

In any case, I promise you that the Beckham is worth a visit. It is a wonderful part of Mineola's – and the railroad's – incredible past.

The Beckham Hotel
115 East Commerce Street
Mineola, Texas 75773
432.553.6506
www.beckhamhotel.com

A Few Words in Closing

Well, we've explored many of the haunts of Tyler and the surrounding area, and looked at many stories of the strange and the supernatural. We're happy that you chose to accompany us on this journey, and it is our sincerest hope that you had as much fun as we did on the journey.

Along with Tyler, wonderful towns such as Mineola, Longview, Kilgore, Gilmer, Henderson, Jacksonville, Palestine and Athens all provided beautiful backdrops in our travels to investigate the tales of the unknown. There are things that we hope you don't encounter – the Pig Man of the Trace, any of the UFOs that have been visiting the East Texas area, and of course, bigfoot – a creature that has scared the people who have encountered the legendary beast.

By the same token, it would actually be quite interesting to run across one of the spirits in the lobby of the Beckham Hotel, or on the dirt pathways of Camp Ford, or on the sacred ground of the Killough Monument.

If you're curious, and brave, enough to venture into one of the cemeteries that we've written about – Wood-Verner, Barron-Shackelford, New Bethel, Pirtle, Danville, Jacksonville, and the others, have a good time exploring them. Do remember that you're on sacred ground, however, and show respect and reverence. As the old saying goes, take nothing but photographs with you, and leave nothing but footprints behind.

As we close out this book, it's a melancholy feeling. There are places that have a bit of supernatural activity that we didn't, or couldn't, write about for one reason or another. Perhaps we'll re-visit them at some future time. Keep your eyes open, not just at the places that we've mentioned, but wherever you are. The truth is that the supernatural is all around us all the time and all you have to do is pay attention.

About the Authors

George Jones lives by the philosophy of "don't waste a minute of your life doing something you don't enjoy." In following this ideal, he has filled his life to the brim with more activities than most people would ever think to attempt. He has written four books, three screenplays, four theatrical plays, eight murder mystery scripts, and several bits of poetry. He has owned a dinner theater and has directed many performances.

George has directed two feature films and one short film, and managed to find time to act for stage, TV, and film. In his time here on planet Earth, he has also owned two book and music stores, and a production company. He currently lives in Tyler, TX with his family and conducts a variety of tours in and around his community and produces events such as a Vinyl Record Show in the Winter, a Paranormal Conference in the Spring, a Writer's Conference and a Native American Pow Wow in the Summer, and a Comic Book/ Horror/SciFi Convention in the Fall.

George wishes to thank God, his family, friends, and the wonderful people who own the places mentioned in this book, and especially the ladies of the Chamber of Commerce and the Convention and Visitors Bureau for all they do to tirelessly promote him and the great city of Tyler!

Mitchel Whitington has enjoyed a life-long interest in the supernatural. Back in elementary school, the *Weekly Reader* Company would regularly offer paperbacks for sale to students; there was always one weird kid who ordered every book on the subject of the supernatural and the strange. If you ever wondered what happened to that kid, look no further... it's Mitchel. As a writer, he's written or participated in some thirty books over the course of his career. In doing so, he's traveled the country seeking out some of the most notoriously haunted places across the land, investigating, interviewing, exploring, and documenting.

In 2002, Mitchel and his wife Tami launched a fascinating new chapter of their life when they purchased The Grove, an 1861 antebellum home where the ghost stories have been documented back over 100 years. Some call it one of the most haunted locations in the Lone Star State, and many visitors to the house would concur with that assessment... Mitchel and Tami certainly do!

Mitchel wishes to thank God, of course, who created this incredible world and allows those with enough of a curiosity to explore its many mysteries, even the ones that some people fear; his wife, Tami, who has put up with excursions into the supernatural for 35 years so far; his aunt Ann Tillman who is always ready to discuss and dissect his odd interests and opinions; and his co-author George who he approached at a paranormal conference a year ago and casually said, "Hey, would you be interested in working on a book about ghosts in the Tyler area?" As they say, the rest is history. Finally to you, the reader – thanks so much for your interest in this world.

Index

CPSIA information can be obtained at www.ICGtesting.com
Printed in the USA
BVOW05s0546290514

354816BV00011B/133/P